THE GREAT DAUGHTER OF INDIA

THE GREAT DAUGHTER OF INDIA

ABDUL MAJID KHAN

GYAN

Published by

Gyan Publishing House
5, Ansari Road
Daryaganj, New Delhi-110002
Phone: 011-47034999, 9811692060
E-mail: books@gyanbooks.com

Distribution Network
gyanbooks.com
India, USA, Canada, UK, Australia

ISBN: 978-93-7097-074-8 (HB)

First Published, 1946

2nd Impression 2026

Printed at: Gyan Press, Delhi.

THE GREAT DAUGHTER OF INDIA
Author: ABDUL MAJID KHAN

THE GREAT DAUGHTER OF INDIA

AN APPRECIATIVE STUDY OF MRS. VIJAYA LAKSHMI PANDIT AND HER IDEAS IN THE BACKGROUND OF NEHRU FAMILY'S HEROIC STRUGGLE FOR THE POLITICAL EMANCIPATION OF INDIA

BY

ABDUL MAJID KHAN, M. A.

PROFESSOR, FORMAN CHRISTIAN COLLEGE, LAHORE

INDIAN PRINTING WORKS

KACHERI ROAD LAHORE

There can be no civilization in which man and woman are not equal partners. There can be no nation which has not been built up by their joint efforts. There can be no unity for which both man and woman have not worked and planned together, and there can be no freedom unless man and woman march forward together and achieve it.

—*Vijaya Lakshmi Pandit*

PREFACE

IT is impossible to make a correct estimate of Mahatma Gandhi's struggle for India's independence through non-violent methods without an appreciation of the heroic part played by women workers under their leaders like Vijaya Lakshmi Pandit. In her own sphere of activities she has achieved as much as any of the staunchest freedom-fighters in the Civil Disobedience Movements, and in the peaceful administration of provincial governments in the lull before the storm when the helmsmen of India rested on their oars, all the while straining their eyes beyond the murky horizon of imperialism, watching for the glorious twilight and welcoming every ray of sunrise over Asia.

Consequently, a study of Vijaya Lakshmi Pandit throws a flood of light on the current political history of India. Her devotion to the ideals of Gandhiji is even greater than that of her brother, Jawaharlal Nehru, and as the first great Nehru woman, she occupies a unique place in the Congress hierarchy, and consequently this account of her life will prove of exceeding interest alike to an Indian politician and a student of Indian politics.

But Vijaya Lakshmi Pandit does not merely belong to India. She belongs to the world, as she has amply clarified her ideas and ideals during her whirlwind tour in America. At San Francisco she acquired the status of an international diplomat and attracted more attention than the official delegates from India. Advocating as she does freedom for all subject races, she has earned the popularity of an international democrat. Therefore, a study of her life and character will prove of use to people far beyond the borders of India.

Important speeches and statements of Vijaya Lakshmi Pandit are given in the text of the book, and the publishers will welcome more material from the readers, which will be gratefully accepted.

CONTENTS

INTRODUCTION

VIJAYA Lakshmi Pandit is one of the most dynamic personalities in India. She has enlivened the political atmosphere of our country with her feminine charms, deep thinking, and clear understanding of the social and political problems of India. Her powers of eloquence in the U.P. Legislative Assembly surprised even her intimate circle of friends. Every occasion has found her divinely suited to the task in hand. Whenever the time came for action, competence for the task has descended upon her from above. If her successful career as a minister in the United Provinces of India was a wonder, her victorious tour as an unofficial ambassador to the United States of America was a miracle. If Gandhiji has an Inner Voice, Vijaya Lakshmi seems to possess an Inner Power. Oft and on, inside and outside the British jails, she has called upon hidden springs to sustain her in the darkest days of life.

SECRET STRENGTH

That quality of secret strength is not unique to

Vijaya Lakshmi, although fortunately she has a good fund of it. Women all over the world, particularly in India, are gifted with this remarkable stamina to some extent. It is the same moral force which emboldens a hen to attack a cat in defence of her chicken. The great women all over the world have sublimated the same physiological principle into a great driving energy. Although women belong to the weaker sex, under the stress of duty and danger, they often surpass the stronger sex in the exhibition of courage. Indian women in the past, when the males were fighting a desperate battle, have often faced the foe with a sword in hand. Recently, in the Satyagraha Movement, they have surprised even Mahatma Gandhi. But the heroine of this book possesses not merely the strength of her sex, but also the strength of her family.

Vijaya Lakshmi Pandit is the great daughter of a very great father, Pandit Motilal Nehru, who said that patriotism was in the blood of his daughters. Like her illustrious brother, Pandit Jawaharlal Nehru, Vijaya Lakshmi has held aloft the National Flag and the good traditions of the Nehru family. She has the unique distinction of having been twice the first woman minister in an Indian province. Her glorious role as India's unofficial ambassador to the United States of America earned for her an enviable reputation in international politics. Mahatma Gandhi paid her a warm tribute for her political achiements during the San Francisco Conference where she floored men like Sir Feroze Khan Noon and kept the banner of democracy flying in the very teeth of imperialism and fascism.

RIGHT AND LEFT

If men-politicians have their right and left, women-politicians have their right and left too. If Aruna Asaf Ali and Col. Lakshmi are the leftists in the Congress and represent the restless, radical and revolutionary India, Sarojini Naidu and Vijaya Lakshmi form the right-wingers closely behind the Gandhi Group. But Vijaya Lakshmi, unlike Sarojini Naidu, is not entirely among the Rightists. If Jawaharlal is known to be a little left to Gandhiji, Vijaya Lakshmi is a little left of even Jawaharlal.

Vijaya Lakshmi may be called the Madame Chiang Kai-Shek of India.· Each of them has accomplishments unique to her credit. Youngest of the Soong sisters, Madame Chiang is the most self-possessed of the three. Elder of the Nehru sisters, Vijaya Lakshmi is the more self-possessed of the two. Each of them is religious only in the broad sense of the word. Their spirituality is crystal, not befogged by the wits of priests. Their faith in life is not bookish. Their belief in God is not cooked. Their love for the country is not doctored. Each is the authoress of her convictions.

Unlike Madame Chiang Kai-shek, Vijaya Lakshmi is not ground in the merciless millstones of education. Taught entirely at home by a generous father and an understanding governess, Vijaya Lakshmi has escaped unbruised. Omnivorous at books, each of them has matchless digestive powers. Their writings do not smell of foul unchewed fare. They write and speak King's English. A study of their books dazzles the reader. In literary excellence they have few peers in the women's world.

THROUGH THE EYES OF A GREAT DAUGHTER

Vijaya Lakshmi, like her equal in China, has produced exquisite pieces of literature. Her book *Prison Days* is a magnificent document of a sensitive soul behind the British bars. The literary note on the jacket sums up the precious qualities of the book. It reads as follows :—

" Mother India, as seen through the eyes of a great daughter—that is the background of this intimate story of prison life. Family affairs blend here with national urgencies, and because this diary is intensely patriotic, it moves easily on an international level. Vijaya Lakshmi Pandit presents one of the most moving human documents of our times. The emotional appeal is there and courage which flashes like lightning through the pages; but the final inspiration is that of hope: the dawn of deliverance is near. The challenge of freedom is delivered without bitterness but the author is unsparing in her demand that truth must be confronted. India's cause is the cause of all people who must know, and then proceed to right action."

Vijaya Lakshmi has presented a touching picture of the jail life to those who have never seen the inside of a prison. Just note a passing reference to a humbler dweller of the prison:

"The tiny kitten which used to occupy my cell in 1941 has grown into a big and very ugly cat. She comes and steals any food that happens to be lying around and as she is more than starved it is impossible to shoo her away. I find it hard to be kind to her as I am a little allergic to cats and not quite at my case in their company. So far no mice and rats have invaded this barrack but I have no doubt they will come. In 1941, my life was one long misery owing to a family of rats who had complete run of this place."

HEROINES OF HINDUSTAN

If there is a great scarcity of literature concerning the heroes of India, there is even a greater paucity of information about the heroines of India. We do not worry about our women at all. We have never made a serious effort to enter into their emotions, and we have never allowed them any appreciable share of activity in this man-made world. It is to fill an essential gap that this book is being presented to the reading public.

In the first chapter entitled the "Heroines of Hindustan" an effort has been made to present a broad picture of the conditions, qualities, and accomplishments of the women of India in the past as well as in the present. The ideas of Vijaya Lakshmi, Sarojini Naidu, and Aruna Asaf Ali are particularly stressed. It is interesting to contrast the ideas of Subhas Bose, Jawaharlal and C. Rajagopalachari—all three of them have been represented in the chapter. The future of Indian women under leaders like Vijaya Lakshmi is definitely radiant and rosy.

It has also been found desirable to devote one chapter to the Nehrus of India, because the Nehru family has played a particularly heroic role in winning independence of India. And three members of the family, of which two are women, have already died fighting on the freedom front. The names of the martyrs are Pandit Motilal Nehru, Mrs. Motilal Nehru and Kamala Nehru. No other family in India has contributed such a big quota of nationalists in the present generation.

CHILD OF REVOLUTION

Vijaya Lakshmi Pandit is the favoured child of revolution. Like her brother, Jawaharlal, she plays with the fire of destiny. The goddess of faith and fortune have wheeled her through many a slough of life. Her faith and fortitude have helped to keep her at the helm of affairs. Shehas borne the brunt of the battle as well as the burden of peace. A soldier of nationalism, she is also the sweep of the house. The Nehrus have a great passion for orderliness and she sets the house to order with great severity. Even in the prison, Jawaharlal and Vijaya Lakshmi have kept their barracks quite spick and span.

The Americans know Vijaya Lakshmi as the voice of the Indian aspirations. She has been India's first woman minister and also India's first woman ambassador. She is dainty but dauntless. In 1942 through fire and steel she risked herself. She has never thought of personal safety.

Personal considerations have never come in her way. In America she skipped from coast to coast, propagating the cause of India. Next only to Madame Chiang, the people of the New World have never showered such a praise on a daughter of the Old World.

Returning from America a warm welcome awaited Vijaya Lakshmi. She was profusely garlanded at Karachi airport. Leaders of all shades of opinion have applanded her heroic politics. But the warmth of public admiration has not changed her. She remains the same breezy brilliant child of Motilal. The times have played a havoc with her body but not with her soul. In spite of her grey-growing hair and immaculate simplicity of her dress, Lakshmi is a belle with Parisian manners. Flashing in and out of colourful groups, her keen mind and telling wit won for her fame everywhere in America. Did she desire to be a glamour-girl rather than a freedom-fighter, the handsome beaus of U. S. A. would have glow-wormed about her. But her mind was not in picnics and parties, although her table was piled up with a heap of invitation cards every morning. She devoted her body and soul to the cause of India. Little wonder if Vijaya Lakshmi is the idol of India. India worships Vijaya Lakshmi.

CHAPTER FIRST

Heroines of Hindustan

Many indeed must perish in the keel,
Chained where the heavy oars of vessel smite ;
Others direct the rudder on the bridge,
And know the flight of birds and charted stars.

HUGO VON HOFMANNSTHAL
(Translated from German by Jethro Bithel).

Breast to breast and shoulder to shoulder, the women of India have fought valiantly in the roughest and toughest struggle for national honour and independence. From centuries immemorial, sword in hand, they have fought afoot and on horseback in the thickest of the battle. The sacrifices of the Rajput women form a gilded page of Indian history. But the glory of Indian women is not merely a green memory of the past. Also it is a red reminder of the present. Cheiro, the internationally known palmist, has declared in his book, *The World Predictions,* no doubt with some sense of justification, that the freedom of India will be won by the women of India.

It is reported that Captain Miss Lakshmi, Commander of the Rani of Jhansi Regiment in Indian National Army, did not surrender to British but was captured by them in Mamyo towards the end of March 1945. She was interned in the house of a friend where her movements were restricted. Later a major of British army subjected her to interrogatories. She was asked if she knew the use of arms.

When she replied in the affirmative, she was asked what arms she knew to use. Her reply was pistols, revolvers, tommy guns, etc.

"What would you have done if I had met you at the war front?" asked British Commander.

Captain Lakshmi is reported to have replied: "I would have shot you dead."

And who was this Rani of Jhansi whose spirit is embodied in Captain Lakshmi? She is an immortal flame of the Revolt of 1857. Jawaharlal has paid a touching tribute to her. She has set a pace for her sisters in the coming generations.

"Here in this city of Jhansi," said Nehru, "the mind dwells lovingly on that chip of a girl who knowing no fear, went out to struggle and die against overwhelming odds for the glory of India and her womanhood."

Subhas Bose declared in Burma that the Revolution of 1857 was India's First War of Independence. The Rani of Jhansi, with drawn sword on horseback led her men to battle. Through our ill-luck she fell. She failed. And India failed.

"But", said Subhas Bose, "we have to continue and complete the work which the Great Rani undertook in 1857. Therefore, in the last and final War of Independence we want not one Rani of Jhansi, but thousands and thousands of Ranis of Jhansi. It is not the number of rifles you may carry or the number of shots you may fire which is important. Equally important is the moral effect of your brave example."

India has produced thousands of Ranis of Jhansi who have fought on every front of India's struggle for regaining her self-respect in the family of nations. Under the leadership of Mahatma Gandhi, they have undergone endless hardships in the Satyagraha movements. The moral effect of their brave example has astonished the world. One such peerless heroine, the subject of our study, is the indomitable Mrs. Vijaya Lakshmi Pandit, the great daughter of the great father, Pandit Motilal Nehru, and the great sister of the great brother, Pandit Jawaharlal Nehru.

I

GLORIOUS FUTURE

Madame Chiang Kai-Shek, during her visit to India in 1942, was much impressed by the spirit of Vijaya Lakshmi and her co-workers who had organised a fitting reception for her in a public meeting in Delhi. Her very first impression was about the greatness of Indian women. She laid stress on moral propaganda as of greater importance than guns and bullets, the heroism of Chinese men and women, and the great bond of sympathy subsisting between India and China. Her reply to the address of Vijaya Lakshmi and other things of interest are set forth in a later chapter. Her remarkable tribute to Indian womanhood is quoted below.

" I am greatly impressed by the selflessness of Indian women. If those whom I have met here are the representatives of Indian womanhood I feel sure that not only has India a glorious past but an even more glorious future," said Madame Chiang Kai-Shek.

CHARMING INDIAN WOMEN

Mrs. Casey, the wife of Mr. R. G. Casey, the Australian Governor of Bengal, paid a tribute to Indian women at the time of their departure. This compliment is typical of all foreign women who come to India with some sense of sympathy and not merely as Drain-Inspectresses like Miss Mayo.

"My husband and I have greatly valued the time we have been in India, the opportunities it has given us, and the friends we have made here," said Mrs. Casey. "We have learnt much and if I may say so, we have also tried to do our very best for Bengal."

Indian women were particularly fine, and she was happy in the friendship of many, said Mrs. Casey. There were many brilliant types among their girls who were the hope of India and of Bengal. Bright and charming with the grace and beauty of Indian women, they had also the spirit of self-sacrifice and discipline.

BREAK DOWN PURDAH

The Indian women have preserved the high traditions of their country in spite of the most harrowing conditions imposed upon their motherland since the British occupation. To be great in a concentration camp requires much more moral courage than to be great in a palace. The beauty of Indian heroines is that they have been great in the concentration camps. A sincere study of demoralizing conditions in India, with particular reference to affairs of Women, was recently made by Mrs. Muriel Nichol, member of the Parliamentary Delegation to India.

"Britain is going to get a shock when this Parliamentary Delegation returns. I can see the Viceroy's House turned into a college or a hospital, or something useful. We must end this sun-dry bureaucracy of ours . . ."

This statement was made by the only woman delegate on the British Parliamentary Mission, Mrs. Muriel Nichol, in an exclusive interview.

By her work in India Mrs. Nichol proved that she is a Socialist anxious to get to the heart of the problems of

India. She admits : "I have in the past read a great deal about India. I have registered salient facts. But I had no idea...I have seen some dreadful things...a beggars' camp where children are suffering from rickets and sores...children with no education...adults who cannot read or write...I have seen apalling class distinction.

" We, as a British Government, have been here some 150 years. We have to admit that only one woman in a hundred is literate. It is shameful. The progress that the women are making under these supreme difficulties is magnificent. They have suffered, and are suffering under a tremendous handicap that no English woman would be able to understand without seeing it for herself."

"Have we as a Government done anything in a searching practicable way for the artisans of India...for the depressed classes ? No. We have left it too much to those good souls whom I describe as " Macclesfield silk and lavender water," she added.

She further said :

" The vast majority of people in Britain have no con ception what the Indian problems are. No delegation has been out before. People at home do not realise how things are boiling up. Indian youth is getting a grip on the whole thing. When you talk to the leaders you cannot help but feel how sincere they are...how they are burned up. But we as a Delegation must stand outside party strife as much as possible. We have to be as objective as possible. Only then can we get a true picture.

" One of my chief tasks is to convince the Indian people that we are sincere. That goes for practically the whole House of Commons on this question of India. There has never been a Government like it. The time has long since passed for India to have complete independence. In the light of the Cripps offer it still stands. The difficulties of minorities and Pakistan must be reconciled by India herself. The new constitution-making body should be formed and when that is formed the transference of power must be given in an orderly and tidy fashion.

"Keep it tidy. It would not be fair to leave India in an untidy fashion. Having created a muddle, we must now create orderliness. There must be a united India...Europe is too cut up. That has been the trouble...minorities... minorities. The more united you keep a nation, the more peaceful it will be. All must play a part in human brotherhood."

Mrs. Nichol talked with Indian women, addressed groups of Indian students whose ages range from 18 to 22; and she talked with British women. She told the Indian students of the part women play in politics and the social scheme of things in Britain.

She said to them in direct fashion: "I think you have got to break down this business of Purdah."

She told the Indian middle class women that they are living in a state of comparative luxury as compared with middle class women in England. And she told European women that they are living in a "hot-house atmosphere." On the latter point, she said, "It is all very well throwing a dinner party here where you have servants and cooks and bearers. Try to throw one in England where you have to queue for hours for your food—not luxury food either—where you have to cook it, lay the table, serve it yourself and then wash up."

SURGING URGE

Mrs. Nichol said that in many cases, English women in India have no conception of what living conditions are like in England. But, she adds, "As life is lived in England at present, we shall weather the storm of unemployment. Everyone is taking his or her share of the burden.. We are going to stand on our own feet in a way never before. America, I am afraid, is in for a shock. I venture to reckon there will be 8,000,000 unemployed there."

Her final comment was: "I feel a surging urge throughout the Indian populace I have met to date. We must act...and not delay. Yes, Britain will get a shock when the delegation returns."

II

The qualities of Indian women were discussed in an article in the *Careers*, dated April 1944, from which the significant passages are quoted below. Mrs. Muriel Nichol has criticized, and with a lot of justification, the evil custom of purdah which is now essentially on its last legs. Mr. Jinnah has also recently advised the Muslim women to come out into the light of public affairs and put off the useless veil on the shelf of a bygone age. It is clear from the history of India that neither Hindus nor Muslims have any sentimental attachment to the Purdah. There was no purdah among the early Aryans, and the women took their full share of social activities, even choosing their own husband. Purdah came into existence as an object of necessity when the women of India, like the wealth of India, became an object of plunder for the stronger invaders against whom the citizens had no means of defence except hoarding and hiding. When wealth went into hoarding, women went into hiding. And it is a strange paradox of Indian nationality that the Muslims have often adopted the evil customs which the Hindus have given up in keeping with the spirit of the times! Purdah is one of them.

THE ORNAMENT OF MODESTY

Modesty is the ornament of a woman, not only in India but the world over. Without modesty a woman loses half her charm. A rosy blush that adorns the cheeks of a lady at the moments of social embarrasment has in it an element of beauty which surpasses any physical fascination. A girl without a wholesome dose of coyness in her mental make-up lacks the attractiveness of behaviour which grips the imagination of a normal youth and converts her defeats to conquests.

Infidelity is an attribute of immodesty as fidelity is a virtue of modesty. A barefaced woman is necessarily a bare-minded woman also. When Shakespeare said, "Infidelity! thy name is woman", he might as well have added, "Immodesty thy name is infidelity". Hamlet's mother proved faithless to Hamlet's father after his death, because she was considerably immodest before his death, moving as she did freely with Hamlet's uncle, and in fact killed her husband by poisoning him in the garden while he was lying asleep, in conspiracy with Hamlet's uncle who became the king, after his brother's so-called sudden death, and married Hamlet's mother within two months of her husband's death, so that "the funeral meat did serve forth the bridal tables," and it was this height of immodesty on the part of a woman which enraged Hamlet and poisoned his mind beyond measure. It is now an established fact of modern psychology that immodesty sooner or later lands a woman in gross act of faithlessness.

That the Indian woman has been modest throughout the centuries cannot be denied. That the Indian woman has been covering her head throughout the centuries cannot be proved. It is now more than certain that the lightly covering of head not to speak of heavy covering of face which passes under the name of the Purdah System, did not exist in the ancient Aryan period. In those days men and women moved freely and face to face. But this does not mean that the women were not modest. This indeed they were, as they have always been in India, because modesty has been the persisting attribute of the Aryan womanhood throughout the ages. In order to be modest one need not necessarily cover her head because one can be modest without veiling her face before the public eye, and on the contrary the heaviest purdah in the world cannot conceal the impudence of an immodest woman if she is really bent on displaying the low characteristics of her soul. During the Vedic period the women were highly respected and were treated on the platfrom of equality, and took an active part in social and religious functions, because they did not cease to be modest, even though they were as bold and brave as men, wielded the war weapons and chose their own husbands as any American belle would do to-day, quite unlike the parental thraldom of young people that has swooped our India and has blackened our social system and has taken undue advantage of the excessive modesty of an Indian woman. Too much of everything is bad and in fact the present thraldom of an Indian woman, a gross perversion of high Aryan ideals, is directly attributable to the covering of her head.

The Purdah System. the heavy covering of the face as contradistinguished from light covering of the head—is child of the circumstance created by the rude invader, who cared as much for women as for wealth of India. Women were taken away as prizes to Central Asia where they commanded a high price, and the ladies of India like the ladies of Arabia, were forced into the purdah as the only possible means of escape from the preying eyes of a lusty person. But purdah has never been able to fulfil its mission, because it creates temptation instead of serving as a means of aesthetic self-defence and has thus failed most miserably, producing as it does quite the opposite effect and a woman behind purdah is much more exposed to social evils than a woman outside purdah, because screen is a stimulus to the lust of the low-bred people. The introduction of purdah system in India has been a great psychological blunder from its very inception, and nothing but a die-hard tradition keeps this social evil still afoot. A woman does not need a purdah to be modest, if she is to be modest at all. Quite on the contrary, the purdah has been found to conceal the immodesty and impudence of a badly bred-up woman in the presence of her father-in-law, although outside the house she is pleased to show the snarl on her face to every passer-by and the meanest hawker that be. Dare we call this modesty? Purdah is the greatest enemy of Modesty. A genuine modesty is visible in the face and not in the covering of the face.

A new trend has taken place in our social consideration since the invasion of the European civilization on our sacred soil. It is the total abolition of purdah, light or heavy, and in any form whatsoever. It also involves a step further, the clipping of the hair, and the dressing up of the girls as the boys which has become the rage of the American belle. Modesty comes first, and let our daughters and sisters keep up their modesty even if they give up the covering, but a light covering of the head does add to the charming modesty of an Indian lady, and besides it distinguishes our national dress from the common herd of American feminine boys.

III

SAROJINI NAIDU

The foremost woman to enter politics, before the coming of Vijaya Lakshmi Pandit, has been and still is, Mrs. Sarojini

Naidu. Sarojini is the only women member of the Congress Working Committee as Lakshmi has been (and perhaps is going to be again) the only woman minister of an Indian province. Each of them has carried the brand of nationalism behind the traditional purdah into the very hearts of Indian ladies.

Mrs. Naidu is as good a freedom-fighter as any that may be in this unfortunate country. It is a characteristic of Indian women that, when they believe in an object, there is no turning back. They stand as bulwark of strength behind the faltering men. Consequently there is a fire in the utterances of Sarojini and Lakshmi which we do not find in the speeches of mere males with the possible exceptions of Jawaharlal and Subhas Bose. Sarojini said recently:

" It is easier for me to believe that the sun will never rise than to believe that Hindu-Muslim unity will not be achieved in the very near future. It must and will be achieved. It is as inevitable as to-morrow's dawn". She declined to amplify the statement further.

When Sarojini declined to amplify her statement, she only exhibited a true characteristic of Indian womanhood. Our ladies are persons of action. They are not fascinated by a flood of meaningless verbosity. While superfluity marks the western women, brevity is the golden thread of fair sex in Indian homes.

Mrs. Sarojini Naidu, the only woman member of the Congress Working Committee, declared that the people of India had reached the climax of their patience and that the present British Cabinet Mission represented " the last psychological moment " to ensure the friendship of Britain and India in the future", wrote Fraser Wighton, Reuter's political correspondent.

Mrs. Naidu, in the course of an exclusive interview, said, "I hope the urgency of the situation has been, if not fully, at least partially recognised by the people of England."

As far as the Congress was concerned, she added, the leaders were approaching the matter with a completely open mind.

Mrs. Naidu said that Congress leaders were willing and anxious to co-operate in exploring every possible avenue of adjustment and settlement "wihout deviating by a hair's breadth from their ideal of complete independence. Within the framework of independence naturally they will consider all reasonable proposals for the transfer of power and for the machinery which has to be set up in connection with a constitutional settlement." She warned that this would not be an easy period either for the British Ministers or those who represented the Congress or other political parties. "There will be currents and cross-currents of opposition to a settlement", she affirmed.

Mrs. Naidu expected opposition from the Muslim League and "very naturally on the part of those whose vested interests in India, both commercial and official, are challenged by the proposed transfer of power."

" A free India," she said, "would like to choose Britain among her friends if that is possible, but this is the last psychological moment and opportunity to ensure that friendship."

Mrs. Naidu added that if that opportunity were lost she feared—because feeling was high today in India to the point of revolution over the too-long delayed recognition of the right of India to be independent—a younger generation might well refuse to consider even the possibility of amicable relationships, whether cultural or commercial.

"The independence of India is undoubtedly the very basis of all freedom of Asia and Africa," Mrs. Naidu said, adding that so long as India continued to be held against her will by an iron chain, there could be no guarantee of peace in the world.

> " Asia is awake," she asserted, and Africa is awakening. There is certainty of a federation of the coloured peoples of the world with which the Europen nations will have to deal as one unit. That is what I believe," she underlined.

Mrs. Naidu, concluding, declared : "It is, therefore, the duty of Britain not only in her own i nterests but in the interest of a reconstructed Europe to take a far-sighted view of the future and to fulfil her initial task in ensuring Asiatic fellowship and friendship by not withholding any longer from India her birthright of freedom which will not be a gift to India but the restoration of what is her own."

IV

ARUNA ASAF ALI

Another tigress of nationalism, besides Sarojini and Lakshmi, is Mrs. Aruna Asaf Ali. S.rojini, Lakshmi, and Aruna form the indomitable trio to-day in the women's world of India. Aru a went underground in 1942 and the foxy agents of John Bull found themselves completely at sea. In t is way she testified to the prediction of Chiero that the women of India will baffle the British Government when they enter politics. Aruna has come dazzling as a star out of the Quit India Movement. Her immortality has grown not behind the bars but rather out of them.

" It is considered in some circles that the British will quit India in six weeks, but I am one of those who do not believe even now that they have decided to go and think that they want to get out by one door and re-enter by another," observed Mrs. Aruna Asaf Ali, addressing a mammoth public meeting.

The Punjab was fortunate, said Mrs. Asaf Ali, that Netaji Subhas Chandra Bose had given the people a gift—the I. N. A.—which they should make the best use of. The personnel of the I. N. A., she advised, should be taken by Congress Committees. If these people were allowed to deteriorate, the Congress would have to repent. "Shah Nawaz and Dhillon," she added, "should not waste their time in making speeches but should get busy in bringing about perfect unity and harmony in the province."

In the Punjab Coalition Ministry, she said, had to face two enemies—the British Government and the Muslim League. The Ministry should put up such a programme which would make the Punjab Moslems feel that it was the Congress which really was their well-wisher and not the League.

Mr . Asaf Ali declared in a recent interview with the "Associated Press of America" that she does not concede the existence of such a thing as a "Hindu-Muslim problem."

"What I find," she said, "is a fight among a certain section of the people for loaves and fishes of office."

She said she personally did not believe in the parliamentary programme at this juncture, because she considered it would distract the Congress attention from "the freedom struggle to administrative affairs."

"Congress in office should, however, be regarded as a period of preparation for the struggle for freedom," she said.

Mrs. Asaf Ali asserted that the Congress appeal to Muslims "should be to the Muslim masses, instead of to the Muslim leaders and I am confident that when such an appeal is made they will respond."

She said she proposes an Azad Hind Government should be established with the villages as the basis of the constitutional structure and that veterans of the Indian National Army, who are now in the country, should form the nucleus of an Azad Hind army, establishing contacts with the masses of the people.

" The parliamentary programme which has been adopted by our leaders at present would not lead us to our freedom," declared Mrs. Aruna Asaf Ali addressing a mammoth meeting. She added that freedom of our country could only come by our continuing the struggle which was declared on August 9, 1942, when the Congress gave a call to the people of India to drive the British out of India.

Mrs. Aruna Asaf Ali was speaking at a reception which was accorded to her on behalf of the Bombay Provincial Congress Committee.

Recalling her underground life during the last three and half years, Mrs. Aruna Asaf Ali said that they had resolved on the day the All-India Congress Committee adopted the " Quit India " Resolution, to continue the struggle for the freedom of our country. " Even though the Congress might not have officially sponsored the Quit India Movement, we believed that the Congress had given the call and we readily responded to it," she declared. " We might have faltered in the path and we might have been caught by the police and locked up behind the prison bars, but the battle for freedom continued. Forty crores of Indians who had risen in revolt against the foreign rulers were determined to free our country from the fetters of British Imperialism. If our leaders, who could guide us in our freedom movement were taken away from the people and locked up inside the cells, the only possible means of continuing the struggle was by some of us going underground. Our only aim was to see the country liberated and the British rule in our country completely liquidated."

"NEW TRAP"

Speaking about the future programme before the people of this country, Mrs. Aruna Asaf Ali warned against a new trap which was being prepared by the British Government to continue their hold on India intact. She referred to the latest move of the British Government in making an offer of a National Government and a Constituent Assembly to determine the future constitution of India and reiterated her conviction that the parliamentary programme of the Congress would not bring us nearer the goal of our freedom and independence. She said that the British Government had realised that they had to change their tactics in dealing with the people of India. The British Government, therefore, had held out this bait to our leaders so as to by-pass the main demand of freedom of this country.

" Our leaders think that freedom for our country is coming soon and the British Government is earnest in granting freedom to our country " said Mrs. Aruna Asaf Ali. She, however, had no faith in the *bonafides* of the British Government. She asked why many patriots in India were still kept imprisoned and why the police frequently resorted to firing and lathi charge wherever popular demonstrations are organised for the cause of our freedom She asked the people of this country to prepare themselves for a new struggle which was bound to come : " The people of this country should revolt against the British rule rather than die by starvation in the famine which was threatening. "

V

CREATION OF HEROINES

The problem of India is to create thousands and thousands of Sarojinis, Lakshmis and Arunas. Once we have the heroines of this type, our independence cannot be far off. And if we have not enough of sturdy amazons, there is little use that we can make of freedom. The mothers of mankind have the destiny of civilization in their hands. Democracy will have a bloodless reputation only when the children suck it with their mother's milk. Now how to revive the golden Aryan ideals among the women of India? The most conservative reply to this question is offered by the Tamil Mahatma.

The address that Mr. C. Rajagopalachari delivered at the convocation of the Shreemati Nathibai Damodar Thackersey Indian Women's University was full of sound advice. There are some ultra-modern persons who might think it old-fashioned, but on second thoughts even they would realise that it gave the right kind of advice to young girl graduates. Rajaji said to them, " Marry after the conclusion of your studies rather than find independent professions, unless indeed your special gifts urge you from within to serve society without any intermediary channel of the family." Evidently the learned speaker divided educated women into two classes—the few who are exceptionally gifted and the many who possess average ability, for the former he prescribed the service of society through the exercise of their special aptitudes and to the latter he recommended the normal path of service through building up a family. One fails, however, to understand who these women of genius are and how they are to discover their potentialities. The history of the world shows that even women of genius have risen to the heights of achievement only after they have been married to men of kindred dispositions or have found the congenial partners with whom they have worked in harmony. He has been generally a man whose interest has been identical or one who has let his life-partner pursue her own vocation without any kind of hindrance. History recalls several instances of this kind, and it is unnecessary to refer to them. One example may, however, be cited to prove the point. Madame Curie, the world-famous French scientist, would not have been such a great woman if she had not married the famous French scientist. It was her happy marriage that led to the full flowering of her genius. But in every society there are bound to be exceptions to the rule. As some men adopt a vow of celibacy to serve the highest ends of life, so can women. Instead of running homes, they can dedicate themselves to the service of humanity. The glory of such women is great, but they are few and far between. What Rajaji said applied to these exceptional women. It was not, however, necessary to rub this truth in because the woman of extraordinary ability would seek her salvation in her own way without seeking advice from anybody and without caring for the opinion of others.

Rajaji was, however, on undebatable ground when he asked girl students to marry after the conclusion of their studies. By saying so he practically warned them against finding independent profession for themselves. The so-called modern woman of to-day has come to acquire strange notions about her independence. She thinks that economic independence is the chief requisite in life, and that marriage spells slavery. She wants therefore to enter a profession and earn her own living. By doing so she feels that she is revolting against the tyranny of the male in the form of

a husband. Such advanced notions have not worked successfully in practice, and therefore the normal path in life for educated women is the path of marriage and motherhood. Rajaji was right in saying that noble and educated mothers would usher in a better day for India through better organised families. This means that the rearing up of a family is not only a domestic duty but national service. The duty devolves on mothers of bringing up noble sons and daughters, who can be an asset for their motherland. Mothers have to educate their children in such a way that they become good citizens, imbued with the patriotic spirit and full of constructive ability.

For this purpose India requires educated mothers. Mothers should understand mother-craft, household management and the art of bringing up children. These, as every educationist will aver, are matters which require specialised studies. The curriculum at girls' schools and colleges should therefore be different from that meant for boys. This may not be all along the line, but there must be differentiation at least in the matter of a few subjects. Those who advocate sex equality in the matter of studies ignore this very vital aspect of education. They forget that the objective of education for boys cannot be the same as for girls. Rajaji was therefore perfectly justified in saying, "The education that we should give to girls is one that should equip them for undertaking the duties of enlightened mothers, the task of upbringing children both boys and girls, in the critical early years of their age." In other words, the education of girls, by far and large, should be home-centred and not career-centred. It follows naturally from this that there should be separate institutions for boys and girls. There are many persons who think that this is an obsolete view of things. They should remember, however, what even the most ardent advocates of co-education in the west want it to be practised with so many safeguards that in actual working it becomes easier to do away with it. For instance, they want that co-education should be practised at the early stages of children's education. But even there due precautions must be taken against its misuse. So far as co-education in the higher stages is concerned, there is a great deal of feeling against it even in some of the progressive countries of the world. They feel that its results have not been on the whole beneficial, and therefore it must not be attempted. It was in the light of all this that Rajaji said that girl students should be isolated from boy students in the most critical years of their life. If this is not done, there might be a great deal of trouble. But this is merely the negative aspect of the problem. Its positive advantage consists in this that girls can have an education best suited to their needs. They can develop themselves unhindered by any extraneous conditions and they can specialise in those subjects for which God and nature gave them an aptitude. This is what Rajaji meant when he said, "Separate universities for girls therefore are not merely a question of protection and of isolating the girls from boys during the period of life, full of chances of error, but are intended for imparting a special kind of education and for furnishing special tests."

VI

WE DON'T WANT DOLLS

Against this there is the radical advice offered by Jawaharlal Nehru. He does not believe that, while man is the bread-winner, woman's place is in the house. He scorns the idea that the chief delight of woman should be in skilfully rearing her children and serving her revered elders. He does not agree with this ideal of woman's education. Women, he says, should not make a profession of marriage. Her lot should not be one of secondary importance. She should not be merely the "devoted helpmate, the follower and the obedient slave of her husband."

"The future of India," says Jawaharlal, "cannot consist of dolls and playthings and if you made half the population of a country a mere plaything of the other half, an encumbrance on others, how will you make progress?' Therefore, I say, that you must face the problem boldly and attack the roots of the evil. We have purdah and child-marriage and denial of rights to women in many fields. Go to any country and you will see bright-faced boys and girls playing and growing strong in mind and body. Here children of the same age are kept in purdah locked up in cages almost and denied in a large measure all freedom. They are married just when they should be growing physically and intellectually and are thus stunted and made miserable for life."

A great French idealist, Charles Fourrier, once said: "One could judge the degree of civilization of a country by the social and political position of its women."

"And if we have to judge of India to-day," says Nehru, "we shall have to judge of her by her women. The future that we build up will also be judged by the position of Indian women."

And if we have to judge the degree of civilization of women themselves, we shall have to judge them by the standards of Sarojini, Lakshmi, and Aruna.

CHAPTER SECOND

The Nehru of India

Men are ideas that a mind sends forth.
From them to me all flows, yet is internal ;
Cheek to cheek we lie across the distance,
Space in communion binds us in one thought.

JULES ROMAINS

(Translated from the French by Joseph T. Shipley.)

The Nehrus belong to India and India belongs to the Nehrus. The heroic trials and tribulations undergone by the family of Vijaya Lakshmi Pandit since the annihilation of the Mogul Empire in India are only paralleled by the heroic trials and tribulations undergone by the family of Madame Chiang Kai-Shek since the extermination of the Manchu Empire in China. The assets of India were looted by Britain and the assets of China were plundered by Japan, but liabilities of each cradle of civilization had to be taken over by the leaders of the people. The crown and the thrones went to the Cyclopes of Imperialism, but the cross and the thorns fell to the poor lot of the Goddess of Democracy.

I

THE RISE OF NEHRU FAMILY

The rise of the Nehru family synchronized with the fall of the Mogul Empire. In fact the Moguls generously helped the Nehrus to lift their heads above the toils and turmoils of monarchy-mauled denizens.

" We were Kashmiris ", says Jawaharlal Nehru, the illustrious brother of Vijaya Lakshmi Pandit. " Over two hundred years age, early in the eighteenth century, our ancestors came down from that mountain valley to seek fame and fortune in the rich plains below. Those were the days of the decline of the Mogul Empire after the death of Aurangzeb, and Farrukhsiar was the Emperor. Raj Kaul was the name of that ancestor of ours and he had gained eminence as a Sanskrit and Persian scholar in Kashmir. He attracted the notice of Farrukhsiar during the latter's visit to Kashmir, and, probably at the Emperor's instance, the family migrated to Delhi, the imperial capital, about the year 1716. A jagir with a house situated on the banks of a canal had been granted to Raj Kaul, and from the fact of this residence, 'Nehru' (from nahar, a canal) came to be attached to his name. Kaul had been the family name; this changed to Kaul-Nehru; and, in later years, Kaul dropped out and we became simply Nehrus."

For a fairly long time the Nehrus had good connections with the Emperor of Delhi and later on when the East India Company became powerful, the Nehrus enjoyed responsible positions under the Company. But the Indian Revolt of 1857 adversely affected the fortunes of the Nehru family, who lost all their money and other possessions. When Fate began to frown on them, the Nehrus made a move to Agra. It was in Agra that Pandit Moti Lal Nehru, the father of Jawaharlal, was born on May 6, 1861. Bansi Dhar Nehru, one of the two uncles of Pandit Jawaharlal Nehru, was employed in the judicial department of the British Government, and the other uncle, Nandlal Nehru, after being the Diwan of an Indian State in Rajputana for about ten years, studied law and practised as a lawyer in Agra. Pandit Motilal Nehru was educated in the Muhammadan Muktabs till the age of twelve and acquired a working knowledge of Persian and Arabic. Afterwards he joined the Government High School at Cawnpore and passed the Entrance Examination in the first division. At the Muir Central College, Allahabad, Motilal underwent his collegiate course and amongst his fellow students at college was Pandit Madan Mohan Malaviya. Motilal's college career ended with his failure in his B. A. examination but in the short period of three months which he devoted to the study of Law, he passed the Vakil's examination topping the list of successful candidates. After serving the term of apprenticeship for three years at Cawnpore, Motilal went to Allahabad to practise in the High Court. It was in the historic city of Allahabad that Pandit Jawaharlal Nehru was born on the November 14, 1889.

II

PANDIT MOTILAL NEHRU

Pandit Motilal Nehru and Dr. Rabindranath Tagore were born on the same day, month and year—May 6, 1861. The one was a politician while the other a poet, but both of them have served the country in a magnificent way.

Motilal won a gold medal in the High Court Vakils' examination and soon established a flourishing practice at Allahabad. He built a luxurious palace called Anand Bhawan and later on presented it to the nation. In this house was born Vijaya Lakshmi the beloved daughter of his father

After the Jallianwala tragedy Motilal took active part in politics and called upon the Moderate group to join the radical bloc of politicians under Gandhiji. He presided over the Amritsar Session of the Congress. All along he had represented the Rightist Group, but the Jallianwala shook the very foundations of his politics.

After the first flush of the Non-co-operation Movement, Motilal and C. R. Das joined together to found the Swarajist Party for the purpose of entering legislatures to give battle to the bureaucracy from within. He followed Mahatma Gandhi all the same and called him "a bit of a dandy" because of his spotlessly white khaddar.

Motilal was soon dissatisfied with the Legislatures. He soon realised that John Bull could not be dethroned by pin-pricking. So the Swarajist party faded away as naturally as leaves in autumn. Motilal lost all faith in constitutionalism which was hitherto the mainstay of his career. Thenceforward he thought more and more in terms of revolutionary politics.

He passed away on February 6, 1931, when Gandhiji had launched his Satyagraha. He said to Gandhiji :

" I am going soon and I shall not be here to see Swaraj. But I know that you have won it.'

III

FROM BAHADUR SHAH TO QUEEN VICTORIA

The change of Indian imperialism from the Moguls to the British, from Bahadur Shah to Queen Victoria, was effected in the oven of 1857.

" After their first defeat at the hands of the British in 1857 in Bengal ", thus ran the historic Proclamation of the Provisional Government of Azad Hind, "the Indian people fought an uninterrupted series of hard and bitter battles over a stretch of one hundred years. The history of this period teams with examples of unparalleled heroism and self-sacrifice. And in the pages of that history, the names of Sirajuddula and Mohanlal of Bengal, Haider Ali, Tippu

Sultan and Velu Tampi of South India, Appa Sahib Bhonsle and Peshwa Baji Rao of Maharashtra, the Begum of Oudh, Sardar Shyam Singh Attariwala of the Punjab and last but not the least, Rani Laxmibai of Jhansi, Tatia Topia, Maharaj Kunwar Singh of Dumraon and Nana Sahib among others—the names of all these warriors are for ever engraved in letters of gold. Unfortunately for us, our forefathers did not at first realize that the British constituted a grave threat to the whole of India and they did not therefore put up a united front against the enemy. Ultimately, when the Indian people were roused to the reality of the situation, they made a concerted move and under the flag of Bahadur Shah in 1857, they fought their last war as free men. In spite of a series of brilliant victories in the early stages of this war, ill-luck and faulty leadership gradually brought about their final collapse and subjection. Nevertheless, such heroes as the Rani of Jhansi, Tatia Topia, Kunwar Singh and Nana Sahib live like eternal stars in the nation's memory to inspire us to greater deeds of sacrifice and valour.

The Indian Nation was forcibly disarmed after the Revolt of 1857. It was subjected to terror and brutality. The Indian people lay prostrate for a while. The grandfather of Vijaya Lakshmi Pandit, Ganga Dhar Nehru, was Kotwal of Delhi for sometime before the great Revolt of 1857. And he died at the early age of thirty-four in 1861. These four years which marked the transition of India from the Moguls to the British, or rather from the Company to the Crown, were the hardest years for the Nehrus. And little wonder, if troubles and turmoils hurried Mrs. Pandit's grandfather to death in the prime of his life.

The Revolt of 1857 put an end to Nehru family's connections with Delhi. The Nehrus lost all they possessed.

They joined the host of fugitives fleeing from the imperial city. And they went to Agra. The father of Vijaya Lakshmi was not born then. But her uncles were already youngmen. And they knew a sprinkling of English. But this knowledge proved of tremendous use. As the Nehrus were flying for their lives from the clutches of British troops, they had with them a little girl who was very beautiful. Some English soldiers met them on the way. They suspected this little aunt of Vijaya Lakshmi Pandit to be an English girl. And they accused her uncles of having kidnapped the English child.

" From accusation to summary justice and punishment," says Jawaharlal, " was usually a matter of minutes those days, and my uncle and others of the family might well have found themselves hanging on the nearest tree."

But the uncle's knowledge of English was fortunate. It delayed matters a little. Then someone who knew them passed that way. And he rescued them.

With the knowledge of English the Nehrus worked themselves into the good books of the English masters as with the knowledge of Persian they had climbed into the good books of the Mogul monarchs. After the death of Vijaya Lakshmi's grandfather, the burden of the family fell on the shoulders of her uncles. The elder uncle, Bansi Dhar Nehru, entered the judicial department of the British Government. Obviously he knew English well enough. The younger uncle also studied law and settled down as a lawyer at Agra. The father of Vijaya Lakshmi Pandit lived with the latter. And he grew up under his sheltering care.

The grandmother of Vijaya Lakshmi Pandit was a woman of tremendous will. She was not accustomed to be ignored. It is now nearly half a century since her death. But she is still remembered amongst old Kashmiri women. She was a most dominating person. And she was quite a terror if her will was flouted. These traits of strong will were marked in the character of Vijaya Lakshmi's father. The same strain runs through her veins as well her brother's and sister's. In fact a strong will is a marked feature of the Nehrus, young and old, and it has helped them to play a dominant part in the life of the country When Vijaya Lakshmi Pandit floored Sir Feroze Khan Noon at San Francisco, she was obviously exhibiting the strength of her grandmother!

IV

FROM MOTILAL TO JAWAHARLAL

Motilal Nehru was born on May 6, 1861, and his son was born on November 14, 1889. These twenty-eight years marked the low ebb of political life in India. For the British these were the years of reconciliation. For Indians these were the years of preparation. The masses were preparing to fight the new battle with new weapons. The princes had lost the freedom of India. It was now for the people to get it back.

Motilal, the father of Vijaya Lakshmi Pandit, was a posthumous child. Her grandfather had died three months earlier. The latter belonged to the old order of things. No wonder, he could not long survive the shock of the New Order after the Revolt of 1857.

"In a little painting that we have of my grandfather," says Nehru, "he wears the Mogul court dress with a curved sword in his hand, and might well be taken for a Mogul nobleman."

While the grandfather of Vijaya Lakshmi Pandit was Mogul in spirit, her father was brought up in the cradle of English influences. Having mastered Persian and Arabic, he took to learning English in his early teens. He was attracted to Western dress and Western ways. He was wild in his behaviour and chiefly notable for his numerous pranks and escapades. But his English professors were fond of him and often got him out of a scrape. He was too naughty to graduate. But he topped the list of High Court Vakils' examination.

The father of Vijaya Lakshmi was keen on getting on in life. Law offered prizes for the successful, and Motilal took them. He served apprenticeship for three years at Cawnpore. Then he moved to Allahabad to work in the High Court. His elder brother, Pandit Nand Lal Nehru, having died, the burdens of carrying on a large family fell on his shoulders. Motilal plunged himself into work. He was bent on success. And for many months he cut himself from everything else. He became a slave to the jealous mistress of law. But he established himself as a successful lawyer. The aggressive spirit of his childhood was not curbed. It gave him the will to power. Directed to his profession it brought him a roaring success.

The times were not turbulent. And yet it was a fateful period. In the political history of India it was then that many of the knottiest problems stared us in the face. Nationalism had begun taking root, invisibly and imperceptibly.

Brittania was "ruling the waves". The ring of slavery had already been tightened around the body politic of India. The idea of "Divide and Rule" had already been successfully tried by the whiteman. The Indian Nation had long been lulled to slumber like a baby. The sudden, jerky midnight awakening up of the year 1857 had been quietened into another dream. Lord Curzon, the then Viceroy of India, sang pleasant lullabies.

There had been enough of sleeping. The baby was beginning to yawn. The British cradle was getting too hot for the Indian baby.

The Indian National Congress was founded in the year 1885. The late Allan Octavian Hume fathered it with a view to ventilate the cause of the suffering masses. It remained just a sort of semi-loyal lukewarm society, "accepting in a loyal spirit" the baits and the crumbs thrown by British diplomats every now and then. It admired the Government for its "liberal spirit" in giving effect to some trivial constitutional measures. Minor questions like the inclusion of Indians in higher Government services, etc., were engaging its attention.

The Indian National Congress fascinated the English-knowing middle classes. The father of Vijaya Lakshmi Pandit visited its early sessions. And he gave it theoretical allegiance. But he took little interest in its deliberations. Motilal loved fight. But there was little fight in the politics of the Indian National Congress. And so he kept aloof.

Motilal Nehru was even then a nationalist. But he admired the Englishmen. He loved the English ways. He had a feeling that his countrymen had fallen low. And they almost deserved what they had got. There was a trace of contempt in his eyes for the talkative politician. But he had plenty of money. And he lived as he liked.

The father of the family was in this state of mind when Jawaharlal Nehru, the illustrious brother of Vijaya Lakshmi, was born four years after the birth of Indian National Congress.

V

FROM JAWAHARLAL TO VIJAYA LAKSHMI

Jawaharlal Nehru was born in 1889 and his sister, Vijaya Lakshmi Pandit was born in 1900. These eleven years were the eleventh hour of the twentieth century, any they marked momentous movement of nationalism in India. Sir

Ferozshah Mehta was president of the Indian National Congress in 1890. He presided over the Bombay Session.

"If I might use a prescribed, but not unscriptural, phrase," he said, "we might give even the devil his due. It is on the third stage, the era of achievement that we have now entered."

Sir Ferozeshah was right. A growing desire of self-assertion was visible as early as 1893.

"I am certain," said Lord Cross, "that in the course of a few years the Indian people will force us to do them justice."

"We desire," replied Dadabhoy Naoroji, "that all necessary reforms and acts of justice should be spontaneous on the part of Britain, in good grace and in good time as gifts claiming our gratitude, and not to wait till forced, with loss of grace from the giver and loss of gratitude from the receiver."

By the year 1899 things were taking a definite shape. India was finding friends in England. W. S. Caine, a Member of Parliament was one of them. He wrote to R. C. Dutt who presided over the Lucknow Session in 1899 as follows:

"My love to the Indian people, my belief in their future as a great governing portion of the British Empire, and my conviction of their mutual capacity for self-Government deepens and strengthens every year."

Events of great importance were happening in India and the world in 1900. New life was astir everywhere. Imperial conflicts were in the air. New emotions had overwhelmed the world on the eve of the new century. It was still the age of Queen Victoria, and Victorian tranquillity was the marked feature of the English character.

In 1899 an expedition had been sent to South Africa. The former Boer Republics were being incorporated in the British Dominions. Before the summer of the year was half through, crisis occurred in China. Lord Curzon was called upon to equip and despatch an expeditionary force to assist in coping with the situation, and to suppress a weaker nation.

The Imperial Russian Government had made repeated attempts at diplomatic contacts with Afghanistan. Russian activity across the border in the North was therefore aggravating Lord Curzon's insomnia.

IV

FULL-FLEDGED FAMILY

The year 1900 was also a year of drought and famine in India, and the showers of rain synchronized with the birth of Vijaya Lakshmi Pandit. The new baby[1] was a welcome addition to the family. It was the heyday of Pandit Motilal's professional career. And the little boy Jawaharlal, now eleven years old, was glad to have a baby for a companion. She was called Swarup.

Motilal built a new house only a year before Swarup was born and called it Anand Bhawan. The house had a big garden and a swimming pool. Additional buildings were put up. Afterwards Motilal handed it over to the Indian National Congress for its headquarters. It was renamed Swaraj Bhawan. And the father built another house for the family.

Seven years later was born another baby girl called Krishna. Thus the house of Pandit and Mrs. Motilal was lit up with two girls and a boy. The children were brought up under English tutors. They had a merry time in the large rambling house with big verandahs all round and a huge garden. On one side of the house there was a lawn, with a a summer house and a tennis court. At the back there was a fruit garden.

In the course of time Swarup (Vijaya Lakshmi) and her brother and her sister were married. New members were added to the family. All of them took a vigorous part in the Satyagraha movement and went to jail several times. Pandit Motilal Nehru was the President of the Amritsar Session of the Indian National Congress in 1919. Jawaharlal became the President of the Congress in 1929, 1936 and 1937. Vijaya Lakshmi Pandit was a Minister in U. P. when the Congress took over Provincial Governments, before the war drove the patriots into the wilderness.

Then in the cruel course of time, the husband of Vijaya Lakshmi Pandit was cut off in the prime of his life. Her father and mother shuffled off the mortal coil. And the great house began to wear a deserted appearance because the wife of Jawaharlal Nehru also left this earthly abode in 1936.

The Nehru family had staked their all for the freedom of the country. They had spared neither mind nor might nor money for the noble cause of political emancipation when other aristocrats of India were enjoying in their cosy houses. The Nehrus had a cosy palace too, but they laid their personal comforts at the feet of Mother India. Motilal Nehru and the members of his family have fought bravely for the people and those who have died, they have died on the national front while doing their duty.

The atmosphere around the Bhawan is grim. The massive pillars of the building stand silent and heavy. They bespeak of the sufferings of the Nehru family. It appears as if the occupants of this building are busy tackling a huge problem of the emancipation of 400 million souls of India from foreign yoke. They will have no rest until they finish the task set before them. Anand Bhawan is not merely a residential building. It is a contemplative abode for its owners. They seem to have decided to enjoy no home life until their motherland is free. There come a crowd of men, women and children. They are pilgrims from far and wide. After their morning dip in the holy Triveni, they come up there to have a view of the famous building wherein the Nehrus, the most loved family of India, live. To them Anand Bhawan is no less sacred than the banks of the holy Ganges. They, all of them, bow low before the massive structure, have a look round and go away. Nobody interrogated them for trespassing the premises. The building like its occupants belongs to the public.

IV

MAGNIFICENT MEMORIES

There have existed closest ties of affection among the members of the Nehru family during all these stormy years in the history of India. And these have helped them to weather all difficulties bravely and fearlessly. They have not lost temper in the worst days inside and outside the British prisons.

"Jawaharlal," writes Krishna, the younger sister, "has one unfailing quality, no matter where he is, in prison or outside, however busy, tired or weary he may be, he seldom forgets a birthday anniversary or any other important occasion. It is these little acts of thoughtfulness of his that endear him so deeply to those who know him."

Jawahar wrote from prison :

"It has recently occurred to me that the British Government by issuing an order under section 144 on me and by subsequently arresting me on the 19th October forget a most important event on that day—and the beautiful and artistic gift that I should have made to my dearly beloved sister, did not materialise—this lapse on my part was most unfortunate. But I hasten to correct it. Therefore, take yourself to a bookshop and choose some volumes containing wisdom of the ancients, and the faith of the middle ages and the scepticism of the present and the glimpses of the glory that is to be and take them and pay for them and consider them the belated, but loving gift of some loving but absent minded brother who thinks often of his little sister. And read these chosen volumes and out of them construct a magic city, full of dreams, castles and flowering gardens and running brooks, where beauty and happiness dwell and the ills that this sorry world of ours suffers from can gain no admittance—and life will then become one long and happy endeavour, a ceaseless adventure to build this city of magic and drive away all the ugliness and misery around us".

Jawahar Lal once wrote :

" You write of 1928 and of our compact family then. Now many of our beloved ones are dead and the other scattered and isolated, unable even to see each other. That lesson is repeated in each generation through personal experience. Integration follows disintegration, but each integration is perhaps on a higher level than the previous one, for it carries sub-consciously somewhere the memory of past successes and failures. The burden of the past pursues us, and yet it is both a burden and an inspiration, for it drags us down and at the same time pushes us on. Sometimes we feel vital, youthful and full of energy, at other times thousands of years weigh us down and we feel old and a little weary at this long and interminable pilgrimage. Both are part of us and make us what we are and out of that ceaseless intermingling and conflict something new is always rising.

When I was a child I remember our family consisting of twenty persons or more all living together as joint families do. I saw that large family disintegrate and then each part forms itself into a nucleus of integration; and yet silken bonds of affection and common interests joined these separate parts and there was always an integration of the large whole. That process continues and normally you would hardly notice it but when events hasten it there is a shock. Think of what happened in China during the past five years and of the cataclysm that has overwhelmed hundreds of thousands of families, yet the nation lives, more vital than ever, and individuals are born and grow and carry on the tradition of the race and humanity in spite of the catastrophe. I some times feel that we in India would be the better for some such mass experience. Any way we are having our own experience and thus building up slowly but surely a new nation".

It is this noble family to which belongs Vijaya Lakshmi and she has the great qualities of her great brother. For years she has fought in the non-violent struggle for independence shoulder to shoulder with her brother. Manfully she carried out the duties of a Minister in United Provinces. If we compare her with other members of her family, we find that she is but a chip of the old block. The patriotism of her father and scholarship of her forefathers runs through her veins. The iron will of her grandmother strengthens her fabric of patriotism.

It is not by mere chance that Vijaya Lakshmi finds herself in a position of eminence today. It is the result of untold sacrifices undergone by herself and her family. The Nehrus have become in India an embodiment of patriotism. Vijaya Lakshmi, whose character-study is the subject of this book, is the flower of the best Nehru traditions.

PANDIT MOTILAL NEHRU

The indomitable father of the indomitable daughter.

MRS. MOTILAL NEHRU

The great mother of the great woman

CHAPTER THIRD

The Golden Girl

I am the pure lotus,
Springing up in splendour
Fed by the breath of Ra.
Rising in the sunlight,
Out of soil and darkness,
I blossom in the Field.

—AN EOYPTIAN SONG

(Translated by Rebert Hillyer.)

If Lakshmi means the Goddess of Gold, the name is completely applicable to Mrs. Vijay Lakshmi Pandit. She was not only born with a golden spoon in her mouth but she also dished out gold to others.

" I am supposed to be a rain-bringer !" said Jawaharlal recently.

Whether Jawaharlal is a rain-bringer or not, Goddess Lakshmi is, and Mrs. Vijaya Lakshmi Pandit certainly proved to be one. She brought with her the horn of plenty and showered milk and honey on sons of the soil. There was a great drought in the country before her birth and welcome showers of rain followed it.

Moreover, she was born at a time when the Nehru family was at its brightest. In fact, only a year before Motilal

Nehru had built the palatial Anand Bhawan with a beautiful swimming tank wherein Little Jawaharlal used to push Sir Tej Bahadur Sapru who did not know swimming.

Jawaharlal Nehru was eleven years old. But he was feeling very lonely. He was full of excitement only when he was making fresh discoveries in Anand Bhawan. He loved to watch the labourers at work. He had learnt to swim and felt quite at home in and under the water. He went for a bath at all odd hours. It was a novelty.. And the electric installed there was an object of novelty. He enjoyed bathing parties hugely.

I

THE BIRTH OF THE BABY

A terrible famine was staring India in the face. Although summer was wearing on, there was no sign of rain. This alarming prospect dragged Lord Curzon from the breezy atmosphere of the Simla hills to the famine areas.

It was just then, on the 18th August, 1900 that Swarup Kumari Nehru (or Vijaya Lakshmi Pandit) was born at Allahabad.

It was not Lord Curzon's visit to the famine areas but Swarup Rani's descending on earth, which brought rains.

At the time as already stated Jawahar Lal was about eleven years old. The birth of a sister was—a "domestic event". And it absorbed his attention.

"I had long nourished a secret grievance," he says, "at not having any brothers or sisters when every body else seemed to have them, and the prospect of having at least a baby brother or sister all to myself was exhilarating. Father was then in Europe. I remember waiting anxiously in the verandah for the "event". One of the doctors came and told me of it and added presumably as a joke that I must be glad that it was not a boy who would have taken a share in my patrimony. I felt bitter and annoyed at the thought that anyone should imagine that I could harbour such a vile notion".

She was born not with a golden spoon in her mouth for her father had earned name and fame. The costliest luxuries of life were avilable in the family. The family members called her " Swarup". She was extremely lovely. And she was therefore " made much of " in the family. Any one so beautiful as she was should naturally become a darling of the family.

At that time her father had costliest dogs, cars and carriages. As he was himself very fine horseman he had many horses of good breed in his stable. He also bought ponies for the children. And Swarup with other children of the family, learnt to ride.

At a very early age she accompained her father and mother on a voyage to Europe. They also paid a visit to Germany. Jawahar Lal Nehru was at the time at Harrow.

It was then that her father engaged a European governess. Her name was Miss Hooper. She is described as a very fine governess. She had extremely good qualifications. And she came from a very good family. She was in fact brought up in many respects, like an only child. Spoilt sons are in abundance. But a spoilt daughter is a variety in India. Friends of the family, therefore, expressed their anxiety. They predicted difficulties for her.

II

RIDING TO POWER

One day a rich client of her father, who saw her out for a ride. He was much perturbed.

"Why," he asked her father, "is it necessary for her to have this freedom, to be in the charge of an English governess and to be educated as if she were a boy ?"

The old gentleman's vision, like that of others of his age and generation, was limited. No doubt he was fond of her. But as he knew that she would be married in some rich family, she would have plenty of leisure and wealth. Where was therefore the necessity for her to labour on her books ? According to his conception studies were necessary only to enable one to earn ones living.

Years have rolled when the old man gave the above-quoted remarks. But even to-day there linger on a class of orthodox men and women. They do not look upon the education of women with favour.

Vijaya Lakshmi envisaged the same outlook when she observed : "To-day, as I sit in the Legislative Assembly, I see the son of the old gentleman, who criticized my method of education sitting opposite to me. He has, I am afraid, not progressed with the times and I have a suspicion that he disapproves of me in the new role (of a minister) just as his father did in the past."

Her father too in those days did not approve of his children going to a public school. The requirements for a young lady in those days were to play the piano, carry on a conversation, mix well in society, and have regular lessons from a tutor. Swarup, therefore, in conformity with the conventions of the aristocracy, did not go to school. But she was given a home education. This her parents thought would suit her future. The future envisaged for her at the time was the same old, "home kitchen and childern" affair only with a little more leisure and a little more wealth. Who could possibly at that time foretell that she would sit in the chair of the Minister for Local-Self-Government of her province and would take America by storm in the presentation of India's case. Her parents therefore engaged for her a resident European governess. She took her out. And she looked to her other personal needs. Besides the governess, for various subjects, a series of masters were employed. They came up one after the other in turn. And they worked the little girl to a dogged dullness.

There was a clock-like regularity in her childhood. In the morning she was taken out for a ride on "a very beautiful white pony with a long tail ?" She was made to ride round a ring which had been specially made in the grounds of the palatial Swaraj Bhawan.

Lessons, play and other activities went on with prefect regularity in the spacious and beautiful gardens of their residence. Every year summer was spent in the hills. And life was sheltered and secure. It was uneventful, if not dull.

III

DO'S AND DON'TS

In spite of the apparent atmosphere of "freedom" enjoyed by her, there was quite a big number of "don'ts" in her life. She seldom saw cinema as films were strictly prohibited by her governess.

She also developed intense passion for dancing. At this time her age was about 15 years. The passion, however, was "nipped in the bud" by her parents.

As her father had come in the political limelight, their house was the meeting place of all the eminent personalities of India. She used to entertain them with other members of the family. And thus at a very early age she came in contact with all great men and women of India.

Here are some of DON'TS which must have been enforced upon parents and childern in the illustrious family of the Nehrus :

Don't say " You're too young to understand."

Don't frighten your child with threats of what father will do when he comes home.

Don't " bawl out " your child in front of his friends or the neighbours, for some little mistake.

Don't tell your child everything he does is terrible. Encourage him instead.

Don't make promises unless they can be kept.

Don't push your child socially or scholastically.

Don't turn on the radio or get in an argument, when your child is doing his homework.

Don't laugh at your child's ideas or you will lose his confidence.

Don't be a killjoy or a wet blanket in the home.

Don't choose all your daughter's clothes—help her to choose them.

Don't make an older child take younger ones along every time he goes somewhere.

Don't keep your childern at home all the time—how do you think they will learn social behaviour ?

Don't set a hard-and-fast time-limit—it's horribly embarrassing to have to be the first to break up every party.

Don't veto all your child's suggestions without investigating them.

Don't be rude to your child, or tease him.

Don't be an " I-told-you-so" parent. It's much better to be the "I ' m sorry—you—made—that—mistake"

IV

GOLDEN HEAD BY GOLDEN HEAD

When I think of the two Nehru sisters, I am reminded of the two sisters described by Rossetti in a supernatural poem as " Golden head by golden head". This impression is emphasized by one of the photos in the book *With No Regrets* by Krishna Hatheesingh—a photo in which the two babies, Swarup and Krishna, have their heads joined together in an affectionate embrace.

Krishna, the sister of Swarup (Vijaya Lakshmi) was born in 1907. It was a bitterly cold night of November when another baby companion was added to the playful company of Jawahar and Swarup. If two is a company, three is also not a crowd in the realm of a palace.

Krishna describes her birth touchingly. She is proud to have been born " in the sacred city of Prayaga"—modern Allahabad. The whole house was lit up brightly (as if she knew !). It hummed with activity no doubt. Mrs. Motilal was having rather a bad time. Everybody anxiously awaited the birth of the new baby. After a great deal of trouble Krishna was born. It was a big fat healthy infant. But she almost cost her little frail mother her life. For weeks the mother hovered between life and death. Krishna was left to the tender mercies of nurses. She thrived bravely.

" My brother Jawahar is eighteen years older than I and my sister is seven years older", says Mrs. Krishna Hatheesingh."

The English governess who looked after Swarup also took charge of Krishna. There were relations almost always staying with the Nehru children. Swarup and Krishna enjoyed them having to play with. In spite of all his work, father found time to spend a few minutes with every child. He saw that everyone was comfortable and happy.

" He was like a shepherd," says Krishna, "who though apparently unconcerned, kept a vigilant eye on all his flock and he did it to perfection."

It is now revealed by Krishna that Jawaharlal had a little brother, but he did not survive. And the mother could not reconcile herself to the loss. The birth of the next girl—Krishna sorely disappointed the mother. But to father it made little difference. Comparing her character with Swarup, Krishna says that she was an obstinate girl. She resented the authority of her governess. Krishna had a wild temper which often got the better of her. Her temper was quick but fleeting. It seldom lasted for a long time. And it held no malice.

" To be punished, locked up alone or be deprived of my supper," says Krishna," was a frequent occurrence with me but it rarely happened to my sister (Mrs. Vijaya Lakshmi Pandit). She was always obedient and docile, most probably because it was less troublesome to obey than to disobey."

Again Krishna writes about her sister that she was "very lovely and was spoilt by everybody." But somehow Krishna was never jealous of Swarup.

" I took it for granted," she says, "that anyone so beautiful as she was, should naturally be much made of, and I was exceedingly fond of her."

A great sense of regularity was enforced upon the children. From awaking to sleeping everything was planned for them. Early in the morning they went out for a ride. Then they had lessons with the governess in a corner of the big garden. Then followed the lunch. After lunch there was rest. " A most annoying thing", says Krishna. Then there was a piano lesson. In the evening they went out for a drive as in the morning they went out for riding.

" Jawahar, Swarup and I", says Krishna, "learnt to ride almost as soon as we learnt to walk and we were all very fond of it, though we rarely get a chance to ride now."

The sisters usually had dull evenings. Cinema was not in fashion. And they were rarely permitted to see one. They had only an occasional visit to circus or fair. Sometimes they had a few friends to play with. Usually they roamed about the spacious grounds of the house. They wondered a great deal about life, and their heads were aching with questions but they had to suppress their curiosity, because they were taught that. "Children should be seen and not heard, and being inquisitive and asking too many questions was a sign of bad manners."

Vijaya Lakshmi was five years old when she had gone to England with her parents. And it was there that they had engaged Miss Hooper for her. Krishna refers to Miss Hooper as follows :

" She was a very fine person with extremely good qualifications and came from a very good family. She belonged to the old school which believed in stern discipline and unswerving obedience. Swarup was easy to handle, but I had inherited all the stubbornness not only of my father but also of a long line of ancestors, and was quite a problem."

No doubt, the blood-and-iron of her grandmother ran in the veins of Krishna ! But the wilfulness of Swarup was curbed through self-discipline. It does not mean that the family traits were killed in Swarup. Only they had taken a more advantageous turn. Time has proved that Self-control is superior to Stubbornness, because Swarup has achieved better results in life than Krishna.

Mahatma Gandhi said once that steam when offered a tiny outlet becomes a mighty power and drives the locomotive engine, but it goes to waste when given a free play. Little Swarup has bloomed into the indomitable Vijaya Lakshmi and drives the engine of patriotism to its destined goal of Complete Independence, but Little Krishna is only a Mrs. Krishna Hatheesingh, letting out a strong steam of nationalism, but unable to harness it to any strong motive in any strong direction !

There is another lesson to learn. Victorian orthodox discipline was infinitely better than modern wayward outlook on life. Previously leaders were made, but now they are only found by a stroke of luck.

CHAPTER FOURTH

The Girl goes to Congress

My beauty is not wine to me,
For I have eyes of languor,
And balance like music
And am nobly born.

IBN AL'ARABI.

(Translated from the Arabian by E. Powys Mathers).

The Congress and the Muslim League came together at Bombay as the Ganges and Jumna meet at Allahabad. So Vijaya Lakshmi travelled with her father from Allahabad to Bombay, because the Nehru patriots go wherever the rivers, whether moral or material, mix their fluid currents.

It was the year of grace nineteen hundred and fifteen, and our heroine was fifteen years old.

The Great War, which broke out in July 1914, made a difference on the moral plane of India. Germany was knocking at the gates of Paris. And London was in the grip of a mortal fear. The Indian troops were sent to the front by Lord Hardinge. And they proved to be a great asset. While the Indian soldiery were damming the German floods, new currents began to take shape in India. The British, the Congress, and the League were coming together like the Brahmputra, the Ganges, and the Jumna.

I

THE BELLE GOES TO BOMBAY

In this sunshiny atmosphere, Motilal and his budding daughther travelled to Bombay in 1915. The Indian National Congress and the Muslim League were going to hold their parallel sessions in the same week at Bombay. The Congress leaders were guests of the League and the League leaders were guests of the Congress. So for Motilal, Bombay held great politics. And for Vijaya Lakshmi it held great fun.

There were groups within the League as there were groups within the Congress. One had its Right and Left as the other had its Moderates and Nationalists. Mrs. Annie Besant was reconciling the Congress groups and Mr. Jinnah was reconciling the Muslim Groups. And their efforts were largely successful. The Muslim extremists were hitched on to the wagon of nationalism. The dauntless soldiers of unity rose to the heights of invincible patriotism.

There were talks of even merging the League into the Congress. The best interests of the country weighed heavy with the leaders.

" The Indian National Congress and the All-India Muslim League both have for their goal the attainment of self-government for India."

Jinnah of 1915 wanted that the hatchet of difference should be buried. The Congress and the League should show a united front. And they should acquit themselves with credit and honour. Therefore, if Vijaya Lakshmi heard Mr. Jinnah in Bombay, she heard him at his very best. There was sweet cordiality in the political atmosphere at Bombay. Maulana Mohammad Ali humorously remarked :—

" So rapid had been the progress of the Mussalmans that a mildewed critic from among their own community observed that Lord Sinha, the Bengali President of the Bombay Session of the Indian National Congress, had travelled hither by the same train as his Bihari neighbour and brother-lawyer who presided over the Muslim League, and the two had borrowed one another's Presidential Addresses in order to compare notes. By some unfortunate mistake, Lord Sinha read out the halting and hesitating address of the ever-loyal Muslim, while the ever-loyal Muslim read out the piquant and pungent address of the ever-loyal address of the ever-disloyal Bengali. But, said the critic, with more wit than wisdom, the two Presidents forgot to take back their productions, and by irony of fate Maulana Mazharul Haq had read to his Muslim audience as his own the pungent oration characteristic of the Bengali, and Lord Sinha had done likewise and read to the Congress delegates the cautious and halting address of the ever-loyal Muslim."

The Muslim reactionaries opposed the Muslim nationallists. A rowdyism was determined upon. Police had to be called for. The proceedings of the Muslim League were attended by prominent Congressites. S. P. Sinha, D. E. Wacha, Surrendranath Bannerji, Mrs. Annie Besant, Mrs. Sarojini Naidu, Madan Mohan Malaviya, B. G Horniman, Mahatma Gandhi and Motilal were present at the session as visiting guests. Perhaps Swarup also accompanied her daddy.

The League gesture produced a wholesome effect. Bombay was blessed with a friendly atmosphere. And the friendship was availed of. A serious issue was in the offing. The League was in a conciliatory mood. The Hindu opinion was galvanized. Mahatma Gandhi had recently returned from Africa. And he was busy in his own sphere. He was reclaiming the extremists back into the Congress. Gandhi succeeded where Besant had failed. The Constitution of the Congress was suitably altered. It was followed by a hearty response. Tilak entered the Congress by the partially opened door.

But Vijaya Lakshmi was not impressed by the political mumbo-jumbo. She could not understand the theatricals.

"Congress in 1915," she tells us, "was a stylish affair. One wore one's prettiest clothes and had a good time meeting people from other parts of India and going to parties."

II

GREAT LITTLE EVENTS

To the great misfortune of the children of the Nehru family, Miss Hooper, their governess, after twelve long years of service, fell in love with an English friend of hers. She later on married. Swarup was 17 years of age. But she still needed a governess. And was therefore very sad.

From thence onwards begins the political history of the Nehru family. It brought about the metamorphosis of Vijaya Lakshmi too. She had till then been carefully sheltered from the world of struggle. She had no knowledge of the world that is "out there" in India. Then she was awakened to the truths of life. It brought about a remarkable change in her. The world of European governesses and the pony rides, was saying good-bye for ever. Up there was staring in her eyes a grim and sad reality. It was the fact of the bondage of starving millions of India, she realized the horrible tales of repression and tyranny let loose by a foreign government. The Nehru family was on the march. The wizard of India—Mahatma Gandhi—

ushered a new era. There was a great change in the Nehru family as well as in the political life of India.

" Naturally I fell under his magic spell and co-operated joyfully in helping to complete the change in our life, which had begun with his entrance into the family," she writes.

The World War did not affect the Nehru family very much. The Nehrus had everything they desired. The misery of war did not touch the fringes of Anand Bhawan. The Nehru children continued to live a quiet and monotonous life. Only Jawaharlal, with his Cambridge air, was an awful tease for Nehru sisters. When he had nothing to do, he played pranks with Swarup and Krishna. He still maintained his Harrow puckishness. He made his sisters do all kinds of teasing about-turns. But he also showered gifts on them. And he was exceedingly sweet. It was not possible to remain annoyed with Jawahar for long. While Vijaya Lakshmi grew fond of his brother, her little sister kept aloof.

" The only change I found in my household, " writes Krishna about the war, " was that mother went more often to clubs and sat with a lot of Indian and foreign women knitting things for soldiers."

The little lady also noted that father and Jawaharlal grew very agitated over war news now and then. But the most agitating thing was not the fall of Brussels but rather the fall-away of Miss Hooper. The governess got engaged and was hasty to be married. All her people were in England. So father of Vijaya Lakshmi gave her away in the church. Krishna was greatly excited at the prospect of a wedding. Swarup acted as a bridesmaid. But both the girls were unhappy at the idea of parting from their governess. All things they disliked about her were forgotten. They only remembered the love she lavished upon them.

" We were all very fond of her, " says Krishna, " and she in turn was devoted to us."

The wedding day dawned. And the girls were miserable. Everything went off beautifully. Miss Hooper was very much pleased with everything the Nehrus did for her. After the wedding the governess left on her honeymoon. And the girls were inconsolable for days. It was the first heartbreak of Krishna's young life. But the childish griefs passed away quickly. And the girls got used to her absence. Soon they began to enjoy their newly-acquired freedom. They could do more or less as they liked. And they were left to their own resources a great deal.

" Since the departure of our governess, " writes Krishna, " Swarup (Vijaya Lakshmi) had looked after me, as mother was too delicate to do so. She was seldom strict with me and more often than not I did just as I liked. That was less trouble for her and it suited me. I was very fond of poetry and so was she. Many a delightful evening was spent sitting in the garden, she reading out aloud and I listening to her with rapt attention. A bond existed between us that was rare and beautiful. Swarup was my guide, philosopher and friend during those days of my childhood.

That is a unique tribute from a sister to a sister. But Krishna was different from Swarup. She wanted to go to school. Motilal did not like the idea. He thought it correct to have lessons in solitary grandeur. The necessary qualification for a young girl in those days was only to be a sociable creature. But Krishna insisted on going to school. And made her father agree to the idea.

"My sister," says Krishna, "had never been to school and had been educated at home. But I do not think she ever wished to go, whereas I did."

Thus the two sisters have been psychologically opposed to each other. While Krishna is father's child with all his dominating qualities, Swarup is essentially the daughter of her mother and inherits her virtues of dogged patience and inflexible tranquility. Jawaharlal, like Krishna, is also a father's son with all his restlessness for a just cause. Thus Vijaya Lakshmi Pandit stands a bit apart from her brother as well as her sister.

III

BROTHER'S MARRIAGE

The marriage of a brother is the sweetest event in the life of a girl. Sweetness knows no bounds when the brother happens to be of the qualities of Jawaharlal. And Jawaharlal's marriage was the first among the new generation of Nehrus.

The brother disposes off the greatest event of his life in two sentences. But sister's description of the same event is more elaborate.

"My marriage took place in 1916 in the city of Delhi," says Jawaharlal. "It was on the Vasanta Panchami day which heralds the coming of spring in India."

How prosaic! It is a scorched spot in the picturesque landscape of Nehru's *Autobiography*. Even Gandhi in *My Experiments With Truth* is more poetic about his marriage. But listen to description of Krishna Hatheesingh in her *With No Regrets* :—

"In 1916 Jawahar got married. For months preparations had been going on, for the wedding was to be held with great pomp and splendour. The house was full of jewellers, merchants and tailors coming in and out throughout the day, and numerous clerks were busy planning out details making arrangements.

" The marriage was to take place in Delhi, the bride's home, and the bridegroom's party left Allahabad a week before the wedding day—on a day that was considered auspicious. Father took over a hundred guests with him and we went by a special train which was beautifully decorated. Hundreds of other guests joined us in Delhi. As even several houses could not hold our guests, father had numerous tents put up for everyone and in a week's time a little colony of tents cropped up. It was called Nehru Wedding Camp."

Well, Jawaharlal has told us nothing about this. Preparations for months ! Hundreds of jewellers, merchants, and tailors ! Numerous clerks ! The wedding party left a week before the wedding day—what a royal marriage ! What leisurely times of 1916 ! Nehru Wedding Camp ! What a fortune the Nehru family must have spent on the wedding of a son.

"That summer, we spent some months in Kashmir", says Jawaharlal. "I left my family in the valley and, together with a cousin of mine, wandered for several weeks in the mountains and went up the Ladakh Road."

So it was here that Vijaya Lakshmi was enjoying herself in the valley of Kashmir. It is her fatherland. And after centuries she returned to pay a visit to the land of her forefathers. She must have enjoyed immensely the rich verdant mountain sides. She appreciated the luxury of the narrow bottom valley flanked by gleaming snow-covered tops.

Jawaharlal went higher up. Little glaciers crept down to meet him. There were not even trees or vegetation to keep him company. He had a local shepherd for a guide. They crossed and climbed, roping themselves up. The glaciers were terribly slippery. They were fagged out. And every step meant a special effort.

Jawaharlal made a handsome husband. " Kamala ", says Krishna, " was one of the loveliest brides I have ever seen." Swarup and Krishna were very fond of the new young girl that entered their lives. They formed an excellent company. Now Jawaharlal had to face not two girls but three.

Indira, the only daughter of Jawaharlal, was born in November 1917. Thus a new toy of sport was flung in Anand Bhawan and the life of the Nehrus was lit up by the new comer from the unknown regions.

IV

NEHRUS ON THE MARCH

Under the influence of Mahatma Gandhi the family began drifting towards practical politics. In 1919 Gandhiji paid a visit to Allahabad. He had some important discussions with Pandit Moti Lal Nehru. The inhuman happenings of the Jallianwala Bagh at Amritsar had left an indelible impressions on the mind of Lakshmi's father. He contemplated plunging in politics. That was the need of the hour. Before that he had been in the fold of the Moderates but the Jallianwala Bagh tragedy changed his outlook. He realized that in a country like India, so completely in bondage of a foreign bureaucracy, notorious in the world for its diplomacy, an arm-chair politician could not make much headway.

Jawaharlal Nehru, since he had come back from England, was devoting more and more of his time to politics. The subjection of the teeming millions was engaging his whole attention. Pandit Moti Lal Nehru was a little stand-offish in life. But for Jawahar Lal's dashing and daring determination, he would have probably remained untouched in Indian politics.

In the beginning Moti Lal Ji is even advised by Jawahar Lal to beware of radical politics and not to court arrest. Arrest in those days was more fearful than it is now. In the beginning there also ensued a clash of political ideologies between the father and the son. It was the natural clash between Youth and Age. Father's unfathomable love for his only son, goaded him to dissuade the fiery youngman from the stormy and dangerous path of Indian politics.

For many days a conflict took place in both by Jawahar's and father's minds. There were long discussions and some times hot words. Both spent tortured days and nights trying each in his own way to convince the other. Father was distressed at Jawahar's determination to follow Bapu. It was discovered later that he used to try sleeping on the floor to find out what it felt like. He felt that was what Jewahar would have to do. These were most unhappy days for all the Nehrus.

It was the dashing determination of the son, which held itself up. Father's love gave way. Father's devotion for his son dragged the latter in to active politics. The happenings in the Punjab, with the gruesome massacre of innocent Indians, at Jallianwala Bagh at Amritsar brought father round to his son's way of thinking.

The new bent of mind turned into a firm conviction in the cause of Satyagraha. At last he decided to throw in his lot with his son and follow Gandhi. He gave up his legal practice in the Allahabad High Court to devote whole of his time to the cause of India's freedom. Nehru family underwent the metamorphosis of new outlook.

Pandit Moti Lal Nehru had earned millions and millions and spent lavishly. He never hoarded up money for a rainy day. When he gave up practice, they immediately had to bring about certain changes in the household. It was not possible to live as they had been living. The first thing he did was to sell his horses and carriages. Then he had to dismiss quite an army of servants he had. He curtailed expenses in every direction. There were no more banquets. Only one cook instead of two or three. No more smart butlers and bearers for their satellites. All their lovely dresses and Venetian China and glass and many other articles, both expensive and beautiful, were sold off.

When Pandit Moti Lal Nehru had given up practice at the bar an old client of his came and offered him a lac of rupees if he would agree to plead a special case.

Looking at his younger daughter Panditji said, "Well Beti do you think it would be right for me to accept this case?"

The daughter hesitated for a minute and then with mustered up courage said "No father, I don't think you should."

Father gave his daughter a quick clasp and sent the client away with regrets. Needless to say that Pandit Moti Lal required money those days rather badly.

In 1920 Gandhiji started his Satyagraha movement. The father and the son joined the movement and were hauled up in the bureaucracy's campaign of wholesale arrests. It became quite a habit with the police to raid the premises of Anand Bhawan. Every time they attached some valuable pieces of furniture for a petty fine. It did not hurt their conscience to take away a carpet worth several thousand when all they had to realise was five hundred rupees.

Vijaya Lakshmi had not been a silent spectator of events in the family. The change, however, was not in any way embarrassing to her. It was the natural course. She was no more the " spoilt child of aristocracy ". She developed daring, dash and determination. Her subconscious mind was all along preparing for the coming events. When the time came, she adjusted herself with dexterity. She was born for the fight that faced her. And so she bade good-bye to all the luxuries of life without regrets.

V

THE GIRL GOES FOR GANDHI

Like other members of the family, Vijaya Lakshmi was slowly blossoming into a soldier of non-violence under the command of Gandhiji. The Nehrus had staked their all on the altar of their country. And there was no turning back.

The end of the war left the rich richer and the poor poorer. Industrialisation had spread. The handful at the top had prospered. The millions at the bottom were crushed. Self-rule alone could better the lot of the people by opening fresh avenues. Peaceful agitation was working itself to a head. The soldiers were not merely robots. Their conscience pricked them.

Gandhiji was the man of the moment. And he was not slow to take up the reins of the unbridled masses. He started the Satyagraha Sabha. And Nehrus offered their quota for the peaceful army. And it was the most beloved member of the family. And he was Jawaharlal. In his absence there was little left of the family. When the son refused to follow the father, it was natural that the father should follow the son. So the head of the family was also gone to the untrodden ways of Satygraha. When the males were at the front, what could be more natural than this that the females should take up the arms. Thus Mrs. Motilal Nehru and Kamala followed in the footsteps of their husbands. And now the children ? Well, they followed the elders in gusto ! Thus the whole family joined the march against imperialism.

" Satygraha Day," writes Jawahar, "all-India hartals and complete suspension of the business—firing by the police and military at Delhi and Amritsar, and the killing of many people—mob-violence in Amritsar and Ahmedabad—the massacre of Jallianwala Bagh—the long horror and terrible indignity of martial law in the Punjab."

The Punjab was cut off from the rest of India by a police cordon. A thick veil hid it. There was hardly any news. People could not go there or come out. Odd individuals managed to escape from that inferno. They were terror-stricken. They could give no clear account. Nehrus waited for scrap of news. Their hearts were filled with bitterness.

As soon as martial law was removed, patriots rushed to the Punjab. The Nehru father and the Nehru son followed them. Relief work was taken in hand. Nehrus took a great deal of interest. Jawaharlal acted as a secretary to C. R. Das who had Amritsar, the most wrecked area, under his command. The boy valued the experience very much. They examined the terrible lane where human beings were made to crawl on their bellies.

Pandit Motilal Nehru, the heroic father of Lakshmi Pandit, presided over the Amritsar Session of the Indian

National Congress in 1919. It was a unique honour for the Nehru family. The Great Motilal called the Moderate leaders to the Congress fold.

" The lacerated heart of the Punjab" called them, he wrote. Would they not answer the call ?

" But they did not answer it", says Nehru, "in the way he wanted, and refused to join."

Thus the Nehrus bade goodbye to the lukewarm Moderates and assumed vanguard of the Congress movement.

The first of August was fixed for inauguration of non-co-operation. That very day Lokmanya Tilak died in Bombay. That very morning Gandhiji had reached Bombay after a tour in Sindh. And Jawaharlal was with him. They joined the mighty demonstration in honour of the great leader. The whole of Bombay's million population poured out their reverence.

After Tilak the leadership of nationalism fell officially on the shoulders of Mahatma Gandhi. Although he was already a leader *de facto*, now he also became the leader *de juro*. Gandhiji excited a great enthusiasm among the Nehrus and the Nehrus were all enthusiasm for Gandhiji. Father, mother, brother, wife, and sisters all foll owed him en bloc. And in that army of peace ful soldiers there was the thoughtful but determined figure of Vijaya Lakshmi. She was as quick to appreciate the beauty of the new ideals as her elder brother.

Early in 1920 the Nehrus were stopping at the Savoy Hotel in Mussoorie. Jawahar lal's mother and wife were both unwell. An Afghan Mission was also staying at the same hotel. Suddenly, Jawaharlal was asked to give an undertaking that he will have no dealings with the Afghan delegation.

This struck him as extraordinary. Nehru had not seen any Afghan. And he had no mind to. Hence he refused to give any undertaking. And forthwith he was externed.

Motilal Nehru wrote to Sir Harcourt Butler, the Governor of the United Provinces, whom he knew intimately. Father felt sure that the Governor could not have issued that stupid order. It must have been the work of some bright person in Simla. Sir Harcourt stated apologetically that the order was quite an innocent one. At last the order was rescinded. When Jawaharlal reached Mussoorie, he found that an Afghan was fondling with his baby daughter!

These were the strange experiences of the family through which Vijaya Lakshmi passed, and grew sturdy like a little oak, all the stronger for the storm and the stress which the Nehrus had to face. Now nothing could deflect the Nehrus from the golden path of non-violence which Mahatma Gandhi had chalked out for them.

CHAPTER FIFTH

Crossing the Bridges Together

How will you manage
To cross alone
The autumn mountain
Which was so hard to get across
Even when we went the two of us together ?

Princess Daihaku of Japan.

" Will you marry me ?" said a romantic scholar to Vijaya Lakshmi. He was a cultured barrister from Kathiawar. He had come many miles. And he had crossed many bridges to meet her. In times to come the sweethearts crossed their bridges hand in hand.

Ranjit S. Pandit, the lover of Swarup, seemed to have dived out of a fairyland of literature. We have heard of marriage at first sight, customary marriage, civil marriage, and marriage through strenuous courtship, but who could ever have dreamt of a marriage by recommendation ?

And yet that was what the marriage of Vijaya Lakshmi and Ranjit Pandit amounted to. And the novelty of the match-maker is even more romantic than the match itself. It may now be revealed that he was no less a personage than the personal secretary of Mahatma Gandhi, the late revered Mahadev Desai. And was Gandhiji himself implicated in the matter ?

Little doubt if he was. Knowing the interest of Gandhiji in the Nehrus, Desai could not have undertaken this match-making business without the co-operation of his boss.

I

THE BRIDGE OF MARRIAGE

It was the historic year of 1920 when, one historic morning, Mahadev Desai came up to Anand Bhawan He advised Vijaya Lakshmi to read an article in the "Modern Review". It was written by a dear friend of his. He described him to her as " most brilliant and very lovable" youngman. The article was captioned *At the Feet of the Guru.* And the name of the author was Ranjit Pandit. He was, as Desai described him, a cultured literary barrister from Kathiawar. Mahadev Desai and Ranjit Pandit had been at College together and graduated the same year.

It was through Desai, that Swarup came to know of Ranjit Pandit. It was the man to whom she was later on married.

" Will you marry me ?" He asked, " I have come many miles and crossed many bridges to come to you but in future you and I must cross our bridges hand in hand."

Thus from a mere introduction the friendship warmed up to the extent that they personally met each other. And agreed to " cross the bridges hand in hand."

Vijaya Lakshmi was married to Ranjit Pandit on the 10th May, 1921, when she was about 21 years.

The marriage was a very lavish ceremony. It was performed in the correct orthodox manner. On the occasion of the ceremony there were hundreds of guests, friends, and relations staying with the Nehru family, including the members of the entire Working Committee of the Indian National Congress, which was holding one of its meetings at Allahabad. Also the local Congress Workers wanted to avail of the presence of Congress leaders in Allahabad. They organised a District Conference. Therefore a large number of the peasants from the surrounding villages came to Allahabad to attend the Conference and the city, normally a sleepy old town, was full of activity and excitement. At the sight of this political excitement, the English residents of the town were greatly worried as they feared some violent uprising. It was a strange correspondence of events and dates May 10th, the date fixed for the marriage of Vijaya Lakshmi, was also by coincidence the anniversary of India's first struggle for freedom—the Revolt of 1857.

Recalling to her mind the married life of nearly two decades, in her reminiscences she observes; "the chance was a lucky one . . . . There have been many ups and downs in our life, some of the bridges we have had to cross were shaky, they threatened to give way, but always we have gone over together, and even after 18 years I can still be glad for that day in November when we met with each other."

The birth of Chandra Lekha, Narayantara and Rita Vitasta added to the fulfilment of their lives. But besides the untimely death of Mr. Pandit, the family had to suffer heavily for the cause of the country. In spite of these troubles, theirs was a happy, contented home. An extremely affectionate mother, she has been an extremely loving wife.

But Vijaya Lakshmi has given so much of herself to her country that she has had little to give to her near and dear ones.

II

SWEET MEMORIES OF A SWEET BROTHER

" The year 1921," says Jawaharlal, " was a year of great tension, and there was much to irritate and annoy and unnerve the officials. What was actually happening was bad enough, but what was imagined was far worse. I remember an instance which illustrates this riot of the imagination. My sister Swarup's wedding, which was taking place at Allahabad, was fixed on the 10th May 1921, the actual date having been calculated, as usual on such occasions, by a reference to the Samvat calendar, and an auspicious day chosen. Gandhiji and a number of leading Congressmen, including the Ali Brothers, had been invited, and to suit their convenience, a meeting of the Congress Working Committee was fixed at Allahabad about that time. The local Congressmen wanted to profit by the presence of famous leaders from outside, and so they organised a district conference on a big scale, expecting a large number of peasants from the surrounding areas.

" There was a great deal of bustle and excitement in Allahabad on account of these political gatherings. This had a remarkable effect on the nerves of some people. I learnt one day through a barrister friend that many English people were thoroughly upset and expected some sudden upheaval in the city. They distrusted their Indian servants, and carried about revolvers in their pockets. It was also said privately that the Allahabad Fort was kept in readiness for the English colony to retire there in case of need. I was much surprised and could not possibly make out why any one should contemplate the possibility of a rising in the sleepy and peaceful city of Allahabad just when the very apostle of non-violence was going to visit us. Oh, it was said, May 10th (the day accidentally fixed for my sister's marriage) was the anniversary of the outbreak of the Mutiny at Meerut in 1857 and this was going to be celebrated !"

Howsoever be it, it is indeed great honour to be married on the day of the anniversary of the Revolt of 1857, because revolt against the established tyranny is in the very blood of

Vijaya Lakshmi. It is all the greater honour, almost showered by the hand of destiny, that this happened by chance.

The meeting together of all the great Congress leaders to celebrate the marriage of Lakshmi and Pandit is in itself a a great honour. Was Mahadev Desai, the bridge-builder, with Gandhiji ? No doubt, he was.

III

SWEET MEMORIES OF A SWEET SISTER

Besides marrying Vijaya Lakshmi with a lovable man, Mahadev Desai also divorced the younger sister from the unlovable meat during marriage days. It shows what a profound interest Gandhiji and his secretary took in the Nehrus. It almost amounts to family poaching by affection. Thus writes Mrs. Krishna Hatheesingh :

" It was during these days that I decided to give up eating meat ! I was very fond of it and one day Mahadeo Bhai Desai (Gandhiji's Secretary) saw me having my lunch. He was quite upset at the sight of different kinds of meat before me and there and then gave me a long sermon on becoming a vegetarian. I was not easily won over, but Mahadeo Bhai persisted day after day when ever he caught sight of me. I gave it up in the midst of all the wedding festivities much to the distress of every one except my mother. She was overjoyed. She disliked meat and would never touch it of her free will. During her illness she was forced to take soups or meat in some form or other. For three years I did not touch any meat though I often longed for it. Then I went one Christmas to spend a week or so with some cousins. Seeing them all eat meat was too great a temptation and I succumbed.

" After Swarup left home, I was rather miserable and lonely. There was of course my sister-in-law Kamala, who was of the same age of Swarup and in some ways she took

Swarup's place. It was at this time that I saw more of father and got to know him better. He too, guessing that I missed Swarup gave me as much of his companionship as he could. I was just learning to know him and love him more than I had ever done before when he was arrested for the first time and our brief period of companionship came to an end."

IV

THE DEATH OF THE COBRA

The fortunes of the Nehrus have been connected, strangely enough, with the career of a cobra at Anand Bhawan. The cobra had the freedom of the house. He was a member of the family, and nobody was afraid of him. He was housed in an outhouse, but had a free run of the garden. Everybody enjoyed his friendship and he enjoyed the friendship of everybody.

" Ever since I could remember," says Krishna, " it had been there."

The cobra molested no one. The servants passed by him unhesitatingly even at night. Often the cobra could be seen gliding, gliding, gliding, enjoying an outing in the garden. No one was scared. No one bothered about it.

"The popular superstition was," says Krishna, " that so long as it was there, guarding the interest of family, no harm could come to our house, only wealth and prosperity would be ours."

Sometime in 1920, a new servant got fright. He was scared by the cobra and killed the innocent reptile. From that day began the material trend downward of the Nehrus. Shortly after Motilal gave up practice and joined the political movement. The luxurious home turned into much simpler abode. Jawahar and father went to prison.

"The servants attributed our bad luck," says Krishna, "as they called it then to the death of the cobra!"

But that was not the case. It was a good luck for the Nehru family to have sacrificed their all for the people. Having killed the cobra at home, the Nehrus were now busy against the Cobra of Imperialism. It was the British cobra that they had to deal with. It had the free run of the gardens of Hindustan. And the Nehrus could not combat with the Cobra of Imperialism unless thev had destroyed the Cobra of personal property. So they took the risk. And they did it heroically.

The Nehrus broke away completely from their past. And they refashioned their lives. It meant giving up of many comforts. They threw their lot whole-heartedly in the new path. And they never gave their luxurious past a thought. They dived deeper and deeper into politics. Their house was no more run smoothly. It was always in a state of chaos. There was a never-ending stream of visitors in and out of the house. There were no more fashionable people in smart carriages drawn by lovely horses, but only dull and drab guests. Each one bore the death-defying determination to liberate the country.

Nineteen twenty-one was an extraordinary year. There was a strange mixture of religion and politics. Agrarian troubles loomed large in the backgound. In the big cities there was a rising working-class movement. Nationalism knit together the warring elements. All were overlapped and pulled together. Gandhiji seemed to cast a spell everywhere. Passions were free from hatred of the foreign rulers.

Thus nationalism marched forward. And the Nehrus marched with nationalism. Father, mother, brother and sisters were all in the picture. And Vijaya Lakshmi did not lag behind. The very exhilaration of the action held them in grip.

V

GODLINESS OF GANDHI

The leadership of Gandhiji soon acquired a halo of godliness. He came to be known as the Mahatma. But Jawaharlal, Vijaya Lakshmi, and the other Nehrus continued to refer to him as Gandhiji. And this mode of address was largely determined by Mr. Ranjit S. Pandit, the husband of Vijaya Lakshmi, for whose marriage the Private Secretary of Gandhiji had played a diplomatic role. Pandit Nehru thus explains the usage in his *Autobiograpy* and acknowledges the indebtedness of clarification to Vijaya Lakshmi's husband who was a great scholar of Indian and foreign languages :—

" I have referred to Mr, Gandhi or Mahatma Gandhi as Gandhiji throughout these pages as he himself prefers this to the addition of Mahatma to his name. But I have seen some extraordinary explanations of this ' Ji ' in books and articles by English writers. Some have imagined that it is a term of endearment—Gandhiji meaning ' dear little Gandhi.' This is perfectly absurd and shows colossal ignorance of Indian life. ' Ji ' is one of the commonest additions to a name in India being applied indiscriminatingly to all kinds of people and to men, women, boys, girls, and children. It conveys an idea of respect, something equivalent to Mr., Mrs., or Miss. Hindustani is rich in courtly phrases and prefixes and suffixes to names and honorific titles. 'Ji' is the simplest of all these and the least formal of them, though perfectly correct. I learn from my brother-in-law, Ranjit S. Pandit, that this ' Ji ' has a long and honourable history. It is derived from the Sanskrit Arya meaning a gentleman or noble-born (not the Nazi meaning of Aryan !). This Arya became in Prakrit Ajja and this lead to the simple ' Ji '."

That the husband of Vijaya Lakshmi Pandit, the late Ranjit S. Pandit, was a great scholar, is undoubted. In fact it was his literary richness which won for him his peerless bride. The very idea of crossing the bridges together has a deep significance. Thus the marriage of Vijaya Lakshmi was a great consummation of two great currents.

Pandit Jawaharlal Nehru quotes, as title to the sixty-sixth chapter of his *Autobiography*—Back to Prison—the following lines from Ranjit S. Pandit's translation of Taranga (River of Kings), eighth verse :—

"Shadow is itself unrestrained in its path while sunshine, as an incident of its very nature, is pursued a hundredfold by nuance. Thus is sorrow from happiness a thing apart ; the scope of happiness, however, is hampered by the aches and hurts of endless sorrows." (Rajatarangni)

Thus the husband and the wife lived in cultured atmosphere. Vijaya Lakshmi's references to her husband are always references to books. Books and Ranjit went hand in hand and they also crossed the bridges together. Thus on October 14th, 1942, she wrote in her jail diary :

" Sent some books to Ranjit. He is somewhere on the other side of the wall and yet how far away. I have such a longing to see and speak to him."

The very next day she wrotes :

"Ranjit has sent me some books. They look delightful."

Thus books formed the chief presents between husband and wife even behind the British bars. Their friendship was based on mutual interests. And knowledge was their first baby. There have been very few husbands and wives so richly gifted. Such a marriage is indeed the picture of very heaven on earth. Complete mutual understanding was the keynote of their home life.

VI

STIFF UPPER LIPS

Gandhiji gave backbone and character to the Indian people. A broken-up people straightened their backs. There was a joint action on a countrywide scale. Non-violence was a new message for the masses. The Nehrus became wholly absorbed and wrapt in the movement. They gave up all associations and contacts. Jawaharlal bade goodbye even to his books.

"In spite of the strength of my family bonds," says Jawaharlal, "I almost forgot my family, my wife, my daughter."

The Nehrus plunged themselves in the oven of nationalism. They began to understand the psychology of the crowd. They felt at home in dust and discomfort. Since they had given up all luxury for the motherland, there was no turning back.

Right through the year 1921 individual Congress workers were being arrested. But there were no mass arrests. The Ali Brothers had received long sentences. The Nehrus were threatened in the summer. But the threat did not materialize. The end of the year brought matters to a head. The Prince of Wales was coming to India. And the Congress proclaimed a boycott. Arrests took place everywhere. The Nehrus, father and son, along with others found themselves behind the bars. Gandhiji stopped the Civil Disobedience Movement after the unfortunate burning of the policemen at Chauri Chaura by angry people. The Nehrus did not approve of this move.

"My father (who was in gaol at that time)", says Jawaharlal, "was much upset by it."

The younger people were all agitated. But Gandhiji was the commander. And he had had his way. Nehrus obeyed him unquestioningly.

When Jawaharlal Nehru, the illustrious brother of Vijaya Lakshmi Pandit, was released, he felt unhappy and lonely, because all other leaders were behind the bars. He interested himself in boycott of the foreign cloth. He was re-arrested after about six weeks.

Nehrus have strong family ties, and they miss each other very badly sometimes. They all have had their jail experiences which are very instructive if not delightful.

" One misses many things in prison," says Jaw harlal, " but perhaps most of all one misses the sound of women's voices and childern's laughter."

" One of the things I most dislike in prison," says Vijaya Lakshmi, " is the lack of fresh clean clothing. However much soap I use, the clothes are always just short of being clean. Motto—don't wear white in jail."

Thus if the Nehrus were to exchange their notes, they can write a voluminous book on jail experiences. Vijaya Lakshmi Pandit has already written a book entitled *Prison Days*, but it is only a small pamphlet dealing with the Quit-India Movement of 1942. There are excellent references to jails by her brother as well as her sister. It will be a rich heritage if the Nehrus could sit together to pool their resources.

Coming out of the prison, the father of Vijaya Lakshmi, joined C. R. Das to lead the pro-Legislature group, but her brother stood firmly behind Gandhiji in his no-change programme. Shortly after Jawaharlal became president of the Allahabad Municipality.

Sir Grimwood Mears, the then Chief Justice of the Allahabad High Court, tried to win back the Nehru family to the British cause, and he offered some inducements which tempted in the past many weaker nationalists, but the Nehrus

ANAND BHAWAN

The family house of the Nehrus where Mrs. Vijaya Lakskmi Pandit was born. The house was built only a year before her birth and it was just ready to receive the new baby. Now it is a national property, being the headquarters of the Indian National Congress.

THE TWO SISTERS

Vjaya Lakshmi Pandit and Krishna Hutheesing with their children

were not to be baited. And Jawaharlal Nehru politely refused the offer of a ministership !

It is important to know the value of ministership in United Provinces in 1921, because fifteen years later Mrs. Vijaya Lakshmi Pandit became a minister in the same province but under a different regime. Consequently, the remarks of Jawaharlal would prove of interest to a student of his sister's biography :

" Ministries," says Jawaharlal, " were going cheap in those days, in the United Provinces at least. The two Liberal Ministers, who had functioned throughout the non-co-operation period, had gone. When the Congress movement threatened the existing order, the Government tried to exploit the Liberal Ministers in fighting Congress. They were respected then and treated with honour by the executive government, for it was something to hold them up in those days of trouble, as supporters of the government. They thought perhaps that this respect and honour was due to them as of right, not realising that this was but a reaction on the part of the Government to the mass attack of the Congress. When that attack was drawn off the value of the Liberal Ministers fell heavily in the eyes of the Government, and the respect and honour were suddenly conspicuous by their absence. The Ministers resented this, but this availed them little, and soon they were forced to resign. Then began a search for new ministers.........

" There is a story of a person who was offered a ministeriship in the U. P. about this time or perhaps a little later. He is reported to have replied that he was not vain enough to consider himself an usually clever man, but he did think himself to be moderately intelligent and, perhaps, a little above the average, and he hoped that he had that reputation. Did the Government want him to accept ministership and thus proclaim himself to the world to be a damned fool ?"

How right was Jawaharlal in refusing ministership? And yet how right was Vijaya Lakshmi in accepting the same job under the Congress regime! How much change there had been in the political currents between twenties and thirties of this century!

VII
FAMILY AND THE FIRE

In spite of the stress and storm of political life, the Nehrus have found a great deal of solace and comfort in the family. They have been fortunate in family relations. In times of strain and difficulty they sheltered and soothed one another. The women of the house—Mrs. Motilal, Vijaya Lakshmi, Kamala, and Krishna—showed splendid discipline since 1920. They may be treated—along with Sarojini Naidu and Kasturba Gandhi—as the vanguards of Satyagraha among the fair sex of India. Proud and sensitive as the Nehru girls were, they put up with political vagaries and set a flaming torch for others to follow.

"Our style of living had undergone some change since 1920," says Jawaharlal. "It was much simpler, and the number of servants had been greatly reduced. Even so it was not lacking in any essential comfort. Partly to get rid of superfluities and partly to raise money for current expenditure many things had been sold off—horses and carriages, and household articles which did not fit in with our new style of living. Part of our furniture was seized and sold by the police. For lack of furniture and gardeners our house lost its prim and clean appearance, and the garden went wild. For nearly three years little attention had been paid to house or garden. Having become accustomed to a lavish scale of expenditure, father disliked many economies. He decided therefore, to go in for chamber practice in his spare time and thus earn some money. He had very little spare time, but, even so, he managed to earn a fair amount."

Early in 1924 Gandhiji was recuperating his health at Juhu. The Nehrus also trekked to Juhu and established themselves in a tiny little cottage by the sea. They lived there for some weeks. It was a holiday after the heart of young Nehrus. They indulged in swimming and running and riding on the beach. But their main purpose was not holiday-making. They had come to meet and talk to Gandhiji. Motilal Nehru and Gandhiji agreed to differ on the Swarajist programme. They could not arrive at a compromise.

"I also returned from Juhu a little disappointed," says Jawaharlal, "for Gandhiji did not resolve a single one of my doubts. As is usual with him, he refused to look into the future, or lay down any long-distance programme. We were to carry on patiently 'serving' the people, working for the constructive and social programme of the Congress, and await the time for aggressive activity. The real difficulty of course, was that even when that time came, would not some incident like Chauri Chaura upset all our calculations and again hold us up? To that he gave no answer then. Nor was he at all definite in regard to our objective."

These were exactly the problems which had long troubled Subhas Bose. Bose had gone to Gandhiji to seek clarification, but the latter did not satisfy the former. It was natural that these questions should arise in the minds of Nehrus who had made no mean sacrifice for the cause of motherland. But Gandhiji did not satisfy the Nehrus as well. But nevertheless, the Nehrus stuck to Gandhiji and offered him their undivided fidelty. But even then the devotion of the Nehrus to Gandhiji was due to his human personality rather than his godliness. On this point Motilal Nehru, the head of the family, was quite clear:

"I have heard of saints and supermen, but have never had the pleasure of meeting them, and must confess to a feeling of scepticism about their real existence. I believe in men and things only."

"Evidently," says Jawaharlal, "he wanted to stress the fact that he did not admire Gandhiji as a saint or a Mahatma, but as a man. For it was clear that this little man of poor physique had something of steel in him, something rock-like which did not yield to physical powers, however great they might be. And in spite of his unimpressive features, his loin-cloth and bare body, there was a royalty and kingliness in him which compelled a willing obeisance from others."

Having known Gandhiji, the spiritual head of the Nehrus, let us compare him with Pandit Motilal Nehru, the father of Vijaya Lakshmi Pandit, because it is from him that she derives most of her qualities. And what was true of the father is largely true of his children.

" How different was my father from him (Gandhiji) !" says Jawaharlal. " But in him too there was strength of personality and a measure of kingliness......In any gathering in which he was present, he would inevitably be the centre and the hub. Whatever the place he sat at table, it would become, as an eminent English Judge said later, the head of the table. He was neither meek nor mild, and, again unlike Gandhiji, he seldom spared those who differed from him. Consciously imperious, he evoked great loyalty as well as bitter opposition. It was difficult to feel neutral about him; one had to like him or dislike him. With a broad forehead, tight lips and a determined chin, he had a marked resemblance to the busts of the Roman Emperors in the museums in Italy. Many friends in Italy who saw his photograph with us remarked on this resemblance."

VIII

TRIP TO EUROPE

Jawaharlal Nehru and his wife as well as Vijaya Lakshmi and her husband planned a trip to Europe. Lakhsmi was on a joyride, but Jawaharlal took his wife for medical treatment.

Towards the end of 1925, Kamala, Jawahar Lal's wife had fallen seriously ill. The doctors recommended some treatment in a sanatorium in Switzerland. In March 1926, therefore, Jawahar Lal sailed for Europe with his daughter and ailing wife. Sh. Vijaya Lakshmi Pandit and her husband Ranjit also accompanied them to Europe. They toured the continent extensively and returned to India with useful experience of Europe.

Then there followed a period of tranqullity. It was comparatively calm, cosy and in a way comfortable. All that she had read, heard and observed was getting consolidated and crystallized in her person. Imperceptibly and invisibly she was preparing herself for the stormy life to come.

As Pandit Moti Lal Nehru used to tell his daughters, patriotism was in their blood and, unless they actively suppressed it, it was bound to assert itself sooner or later.

There came an opportunity—the political movement of 1931-32—for the patriotism in her blood to assert itself, and it readily did.

When Gandhi returned from England to India after having attended the Round Table Conference, most tumultuous scenes in the battlefield of Indian political struggle were witnessed.

When the Mahatma set foot on the Indian soil, Pandit Jawahar Lal Nehru and his comrades had already been arrested. Here was a repressive move precipitated by the Government. The Congress hurried towards a catastrophic conflict. It resulted in the Civil D'sobedience Movement of the year 1932.

The fault for igniting the conflagration lay entirely with the Government.

But to return to Europe again. After the departure of Lakshmi and Pandit, Jawahar and Kamala, the remaining members of the family also desired to follow. Motilal planned a tour to Europe and Krishna was to accompany him. Unfortunately, he had to cancel his passage due to important case which was pending and could not be postponed. He asked Krishna if she would go alone. She hesitated and was torn between two desires. She decided to go alone. Mother was most distressed. She tried to argue with the girl, but she could not dissuade her. So the tomboy left for Europe alone.

Jawaharlal was living at Geneva. He was to have met Kr'shna at Brindisi. Having missed his train, he did not arrive. She was overcome with a terrible sense of loneliness. Jawahar met her at Naples and they went to Geneva, visiting Rome, Florence and other cities en route.

In the summer of 1927 Pandit Motilal also went to Europe. Everybody was happy about it. He needed rest rather badly. A complete change of surroundings suited him. In his last letter before he sailed he wrote :

" You and Bhai (Jawahar) have both been insisting on my taking a holiday in Europe and at this end Swarup and Ranjit are doing the same and at last I find it possible to go away in the near future. I am a bit tired with the public work that I have been doing for the last seven years and it is disturbing to find at the end of this long period that I have failed to advance the cause of the country in any appreciable way. So I have decided to take a holiday and no longer deny myself the pleasure of being with all of you."

In the same letter Motilal gave a significant advice to Krishna. The advice is so significant of his character that he must have tendered the same advice to his elder daughter Vijaya Lakshmi. In fact it applies to every woman who values her life. Therefore, I think it advisable to quote it in full:

" You seem to have turned quite a little politician, but do not think that being a girl will in any way be a handicap to you. Many women have taken as great a part in the uplift of their country as any man has done and some have distinguished themselves much more than men. It is all a question of one's feelings towards one's country and how seriously one applies oneself to the question of uplift. There is no bar to sex—on the contrary a determined woman's influence is much greater than a man can ever sway. So there is every chance for you. You must remember that true patriotism is in your blood and unless you actively suppress it, it is bound to assert itself sooner or later."

This was a very sound advice to Nehru girls. And there is no doubt that they have lived up to it. In fact Vijaya Lakshmi on the whole has followed it better than Krishna, the younger girl, to whom the letter above had been addressed.

After some wanderings in Europe, Jawahar, Kamala and Indira returned to India. Vijaya Lakshmi and Ranjit Pandit had returned much earlier—before the departure of father for Europe. But father stayed on for sometime. And now while father was still in Europe, the adventurous members of the Nehru family planned another tour in Europe.

" During this time," writes Krishna, " my sister and her husband again went to Europe leaving their little daughters, Chanderlekha and Narayantara with mother. As mother was very unwell at that time I had to look after them and though I was very fond of them it was not an easy task."

IX

FIGHTING ON THE FRONT

Immediately after his return from Europe, Jawaharlal attended the Madras Session of the Indian National Congress. He was caught in the whirl. And the Nehru sisters followed his lead. At Madras Jawaharlal presented a bunch of resolutions. These were resolutions on Independence, War Danger, and association with the League Against Imperialism. To the surprise of Jawahar all of them were passed.

During the visit of the Simon Commission of which the present Prime Minister of England, Clement Attlee was a member, the Nehru family received its share of punishment. Lala Lajpat Rai was beaten to death and his death was avenged by Bhagat Singh. But many leaders had received minor injuries from the police in protest demonstration.

" It was in this connection," says Jawaharlal, " that I had a new experience, and my body felt the baton and lathi blows from the police."

It was indeed a great honour to the Nehru family and a matter of great pleasure to Vijaya Lakshmi when her brother became president of the Lahore Session of the Indian National Congress where the resolution for Complete Independence was passed. January 26, 1930 was celebrated as the Independence Day throughout India, and Gandhiji launched Civil Disobedience against Salt Act.

" Salt " says Jawaharlal, " suddenly became a mysterious word, a word of power. The Salt Tax was to be attacked, the Salt Laws were to be broken."

Jawaharlal Nehru was arrested on April 14, 1930. His father became the acting President of the Congress. He was poor in health. Nevertheless, he threw himself into the

NEHRU NYMPHS

Vijaya Lakshmi Pandit and Krishna Hutheesing

WOMAN MINISTER
Vijaya Lakshmi as Minister in the United Pravinces

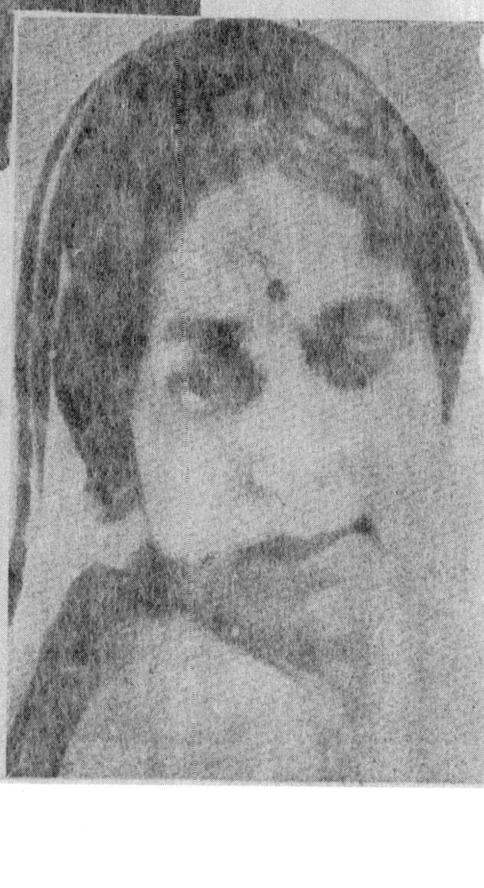

WOMAN LEADER
Vijaya Lakshmi as President of the Women's Conference at Cocanana.

work with great energy. The movement benefitted greatly. But it was at the cost of his precious health.

The country was aflame with fiery patriotism. Gandhi, Patel and all other credited leaders were also arrested. A reign of repression was let loose by the bureaucracy all over the country. The only fault of the people was that they demonstrated their urge to be free from the yokes of slavery. They demanded freedom for their Motherland. Arrests, Lathi charges and firings were common occurrences of everyday. Ordinance upon ordinance was being piled by the Viceroy.

Vijaya Lakshmi responded to the call of the hour. She joined the ranks of surging millions for demonstrating the resentment of the Indian people. She fought tooth and nail against the foreign rule. She delivered speeches. She led processions. She organised hartals. Now she was here, now there. Therefore, a notice was served on her prohibiting her from taking part in the movement for a period of one month. But how could this great daughter of India comply with a notice from His Majesty's Government? How could she keep mum ? How could she refrain from helping the people in their struggle for freedom ?

It happened as it was expected. And she was arrested on the 27th January, 1932 along with her sister Krishna. All members of the Nehru family were in jail except their frail little mother. She was left behind all alone in the huge house. It had once known so much of joy and happiness. But now there was only sorrow and gloom. She was tried and sentenced to one year's rigorous imprisonment with fine. Her younger sister got the same sentence without fine. That year she was kept in the Lucknow jail. Her youngest child at the time was less than three years old. How painful it must have been for a mother to stay away from her little children for the whole year !

The first time she had an occasion to speak in public. It was during this non-co-operation movement at Allahabad. Most of the leaders had gone to jail. Women were called upon to come forward and fight for the liberation of the country.

In one of her narrations she gives an interesting account of her maiden attempts at public speaking. One morning at the end of a long procession she was asked to speak in public.

" I hadn't a thought in my head and not a trace of inspiration could I get from the faces around me. It was a difficult moment. Quite suddenly something happened. The crowd before me became a part of myself. We were both part of some bigger unseen forces ; the message was there, it had only to be delivered. I spoke and the crowd cheered. I was happy in my little success. After this I was called upon to speak quite often."

Her experience of speaking to an audience of students was rather unfortunate. She expected them to be equipped with current information. Therefore, she had to be a little "scholarly" in what she said. But the intellectual glimmerings brought a dull respond from the unmoved faces in front. Ever since the beginning of human history, emotion has been ruling human actions. Cold reason and learning are of a very recent growth. One day it struck her that she should be just homely with the students. Instead of delivering a speech she should informally talk to them. Ever since she has been a success with them too.

In this connection she recalls an incident. Once she was invited to attend a meeting held by a Students' Union in remembrance of Maxim Gorki. Learned people came on the stage and gave complicated details of the various issues. The atmosphere was dull and drab.

The audience coldly stared at the face of each speaker. They waited for the end of the speech in expectation of another more lively. She could not restrain herself. She asked for permission to speak which was readily granted. She interpreted the message of Gorki in terms which the Indian worker could follow. And soon applause bubbled out from the meeting. But after her it was not easy for any speaker to get a patient hearing.

In 1935 she stood up as a candidate for the Municipal Board membership in Allahabad and was elected with an overwhelming support.

During that period she was also elected as the chair-woman of the Education Committee. In this capacity she worked for about eighteen months. She gathered considerable experience of the civic and educational life of the area.

In the year 1938, she was the Minister of Local Self-Government, in the Congress Ministry of the United Provinces. She again went to Europe. Her stay in Europe coincided with the most critical period of European politics. It was a little before the World War broke out. She was in London when the Munich Pact was signed.

Europe was heading towards Second World War, she saw hundreds of young boys, dressed in the Fascist Uniform passing in military order through a street of an Italian town. Probably it was some Fascist celebration. The sight of those young boys, she says, reminded her of the ugly force of Fascism. It was a totalitarian state which endeavoured to rule by the power of might alone. It crushed justice and liberty. The youngmen seemed to her a flock of sheep being driven unconscious to the slaugther-house of the war.

X

NEHRUS' BID FOR FREEDOM

"These were days of stirring news," says Jawaharlal, processions and lathi charges and firing, frequent hartals to celebrate noted arrests, and special observances, like Peshawar Day, Garhwali Day, etc. For the time being the boycott of foreign cloth and all British goods was almost complete. When I heard that my aged mother and, of course, my sisters used to stand under the hot summer sun, picketing before foreign cloth shops, I was greatly moved. Kamala did so also, but she did something more. She threw herself into the movement in Allahabad city and district with an energy and determination which amazed me, who thought I had known her so well for so many years. She forgot her ill-health and rushed about the whole day in the sun, and showed remarkable powers of organisation. I heard of this vaguely in gaol. Later, when my father joined me there, I was to learn from him how he had himself appreciated Kamala's work, and especially her organising capacity. He did not at all fancy my mother or the girls rushing about in the hot sun, but, except for an occasional remonstrance, he did not interfere."

The biggest news of all had come from Peshawar. There a remarkable exhibition of disciplined and peaceful courage stirred the country. The Pathans noted for courage are not noted for non-violence. Yet these Pathans set an example which was unique in India. Even more stirring was the refusal of Garhwali soldiers to fire on the people.

The most striking thing was the part of the women in the national struggle. They came in large numbers from the seclusion of their homes. Although unused to public activity they threw themselves into the heart of the struggle. The picketing of foreign cloth was their favourite occupation.

Picketing of liquor shops they made their preserve. Enormous processions consisting of women alone were taken out in all cities. Generally the attitude of the women was more unyielding than that of the men. Often they became Congress dictators in provinces and in local areas.

The breach of the Salt Act became a national fever. The Viceroy issued ordinance after ordinance. "As these ordinances and prohibitions grew," says Jawaharlal, "the opportunities for breaking them also grew." The people did the very things which were declared illegal. The initiative remained with the Congress. Gandhiji was arrested on May 5, 1930. It was followed by big raids on salt pans and depots.

In the latter half of June 1930 the father of Vijaya Lakshmi Pandit went to Bombay accompanied by her mother and Kamala, the wife of Jawaharlal. They had a great reception. And it was followed by the fiercest of lathi charges. On his return from Bombay the father of Vijaya Lakshmi was arrested on June 30, 1930. He was sentenced to six months.

"My father's arrest," says Jawaharlal, "was probably due to his having issued a statement defining the duties of a soldier or policeman in the event of an order to fire on civil population being given."

The Bombay visit had a great strain on Motilal. Early and late he was kept busy. He had to take the responsibility for every decision. He had long been unwell. But now he returned fagged out. He was packing for Mussorrie when he found himself in Naini Central Prison.

The Working Committee was declared illegal. All members were to be arrested. Therefore, substitute members were added. Several women became acting members. Kamala, the wife of Jawaharlal was one of them. Shortly after Ranjit

S. Pandit, the dear husband of Vijaya Lakshmi, was also arrested and he joined her brother, Jawaharlal, in his barrack.

Motilal Nehru was released due to very bad state of health and Jawaharlal came out after the expiry of six months' sentence. But he expected his freedom to be a short one. Kamala was in Allahabad, busy with her Congress work. Father was under treatment at Mussorrie. Mrs. Motilal was there. So were Vijaya Lakshmi and Krishna. Jawaharlal was planning a no-tax campaign.

"And then," says Jawaharlal, " on October 13th Kamala and I went off to Mussorrie to spend three days with father. He was looking just a little better, and I was happy to think that he had turned the corner and was getting well. I remember those quiet and delightful three days well ; it was good to be back in the family. Indira, my daughter, was there ; and my three little nieces, my sister's daughters (the children of Vijaya Lakshmi). I would play with the children and sometimes we would march bravely round the house in a stately procession, led, flag in hand, by the youngest, aged three or four, singing *Jhanda uucha rahe hamara*, our flag song. And those three days were the last I was to have with father before his fatal illness came to snatch him away from me."

After eight days' freedom, Jawaharlal found himself back again in Naini. In the same old barrack he rejoined Ranjit S. Pandit, the husband of Vijaya Lakshmi while the heroine herself was busy nursing her father at Mussorrie. Krishna thus narrates the family episode which is so firmly knit with the history of India itself :

"Father did not like the idea of Kamala, my sister (Vijaya Lakshmi) and I going about all day in the scorching sun. He refused to remonstrate with us and he never forced any of us to give up the work we were doing. He was not keeping good health and wanted his children near him. Jawahar was in jail and father did not want any of us to court arrest. His state of health did not prevent him from working and directing the movement but the strain of working from morning till evening with almost no rest at all was too great for him. The doctors advised him to take rest. But the government forestalled the doctors and arrested him on June 30, 1930. Thus instead of going to a hill stastion he merely crossed the Ganges and entered Naini Prison. During the ten weeks father had spent in prison his health had steadily deteriorated. It was only when he was a mere shadow of his former self that the British Government thought it fit to release him. Soon after he came out, all of us went to Mussoorie where the mountain air and homely comforts helped to bring back some strength to his tired, ailing body."

CHAPTER SIXTH

The Pillar Falls

I am Lord of the Risers from Death,
Whose Forms are the Lamps in the House of the Dead,
Whose shrine is the Earth.

— THE BOOK OF THE DEAD.

(Translated from Egyptian by Robert Hillyer)

The death of Motilal Nehru, the great father of Vijaya Lakshmi, was the first great calamity in the smooth sailing life of the heroine. It was as if the pillar of the Nehrus had fallen down. Also it was a great national tragedy.

The re-arrest of Jawaharlal was a rude shock to his father. For a while the Great Man sat with his head bowed with grief. But his lion-hearted soul would not submit to any weakness. Almost immediately he pulled himself together. And he banged a table in front of him. He was going to be well. He would do a man's work. He would not submit weakly to illness. It was a brave resolve. But a deep-seated disease was eating into him. And no strength of will could overcome it. It could be crushed, but it could not be killed. But temporarily it worked a marked surprise.

" For some months past," says Jawaharlal, " ever since he was at Yervada, he had been bringing up blood in his sputum. This stopped quite suddenly after this resolve of his, and for some days it did not re-appear. He was pleased about it, and he came to see me in prison, and he mentioned this fact to me in some triumph."

But it was a brief respite. The blood came later in great quantities. The disease reasserted itself. During this interval he worked with his old energy. He gave a great push to the civil disobedience movement all over India.

I

PIN-PRICKING THE BRITISH LION

Motilal held discussions with leaders. He issued detailed instructions. The birthday of Jawaharlal was fixed for an all-India celebration. The offending passages from his speeches for which he was convicted were read at public meetings. There were numerous lathi-charges. The processions were forcibly dispersed. Five thousand arrests were made on a single day all over India.

"It was a unique birthday celebration", says Jawaharlal.

This pouring out of energy was very bad for Motilal. Vijaya Lakshmi begged her father to take complete rest. Jawaharlal suggested him to take a short voyage out of India. He agreed. It was arranged that a doctor might accompany him. With this object in view he went to Calcutta. But his condition grew worse. He was unable to go far. In a Calcutta suburb he remained for seven weeks. Vijaya Lakshmi and other members of the family joined him there.

"These were heart-breaking weeks," says Krishna. "Father seemed to sense that he would not recover and there was nothing one could do about it. He was not gloomy, on the contrary he was always making fun of his illness knowing full well that it was a matter of a few weeks here or there. His courage was superb to the end."

Sanskrit, and he was indeed a great asset to international culture.

II

THE WOMAN FOLLOWS THE MAN

The New Year Day of nineteen hundred and thirty-one brought the news of Kamala's arrest. Jawaharlal was pleased because she had long desired to follow her comrades to the dark cell.

"Ordinarily," says Jawaharlal, "if they had been men, both she and my sister (Vijaya Lakshmi) and many other women would have been arrested long ago. But at that time the Government avoided, as far as possible arresting women, and so they escaped for long."

But now the wife of Jawaharlal had her heart's desire! How glad she must be, thought Nehru. But he was apprehensive. She had a very delicate health. And the prison suffering would increase her difficulties. A press-man had asked her for a message. On the spur of the moment, she said :

"I am happy beyond measure and proud to follow in the footsteps of my husband. I hope the people will keep the flag flying."

That was in the traditions of the Nehru family. Did not Motilal say that patriotism was in the blood of his children !

Motilal was in Calcutta. And he was far from being well. But the arrest of his daughter-in-law shook him up. And he decided to return to Allahabad. He sent Krishna immediately before him. Then he followed to Anand Bhawan with Vijaya Lakshmi Pandit and other members of the family.

Motilal went to see his son in Naini. Jawaharlal had a shock. The appearance of his father produced a dismay in him. His face was swollen up. That face haunted Jawaharlal. It was so utterly unlike him. A fear began to creep in his mind. His rich personality was missing. His overflowing vitality had gone. The all-embracing warmth was still visible, but the shadow of death was lengthening on his face. The mind of Jawaharlal was full of black forebodings.

I was not long before Krishna, the younger sister of Vijaya Lakshmi, was also arrested. One day she went to attend the trials of a whole batch of Youth Leaguers. It was her business to attend the trials of Youth Leaguers, because she was the secretary of the Youth League. As Krishna was leaving the court, she and her cousin were confronted with an arrest warrant for having been members of an unlawful assembly a week before. The girls were taken aback. But there was nothing they could do about it.

Krishna was sorry for one reason alone. Her father was very ill. He had repeatedly told her that he hoped that she would not go to jail just then. She did not want father to think that she had deliberately courted arrest. It was winter. The prison cell was cold and filthy. Vermins crawled all over the place. The cousins tried to amuse themselves for a while. But then they lapsed into silence. Krishna was terribly unhappy, thinking of her father. At midnight they were released, because an anonymous friend of theirs had paid the fine even against their wishes. Father was pleased to see his daughter, but he was annoyed at the fine having been paid. He was furious. He was deeply hurt.

Father's health grew worse and worse. His children had always associated health with him. But now he was a little bent. He was weak and pale-looking. His face was swollen. At last he was confined to bed. Even then he did not appear close to death. It just did not seem possible that death could take him away. He had always fought against odds. And he had always won. Everyone was sure that he would win through. But it was not to be.

These were the last days of first Round Table Conference. The Congress leaders were a bit amused. Their amusement had a touch of disdain in it. The discussions in London seemed unreal. But one backbone of reality did stand out. It was that some people in India were always prepared to play to the British tunes. Under the deceptive cover of nationalism different economic interests are at work. The Round Table Coference was a collection of these vested interests.

January 26, 1931, found Jawaharlal and his brother-in-law, Ranjit, musing in the prison. In the forenoon they were told that the condition of Motilal was serious. And that they must go home immediately. On enquiry they found that they were being discharged. The husband of Vijaya Lakshmi accompanied Jawaharlal to the bedside of the Great Man where Vijaya Lakshmi, Krishna, and others were keeping vigils and fighting against the invincible Death.

III

SHADOWS OF DEATH

"It was the 26th January 1931, Independence Day," says Krishna, "that Jawahar and my brother-in-law Ranjit were released unconditionally as father's condition was serious. Twelve years ago it happened and yet the memory of that day is still achingly fresh in my mind's eye. Jawahar arrived at Anand Bhawan and went straight to father's boom."

Vijaya Lakshmi was there, nursing daddy. And Motilal was pleased to see her husband and Jawaharlal. Gandhiji was also released the same day. Motilal was anxious to see him. The same day Gandhiji started from Bombay and arrived at Allahabad. His presence had a markedly soothing effect on father and the family.

"A day or two later," says Jawaharlal, "Ranjit (who did not come in the category of Working Committee members) was taken back to Naini prison. This upset father, and he was continually asking for him and complaining that when so many people were coming to see him from distant parts of India, his own son-in-law was kept away. The doctor were worried by this insistence, and it was obvious that it was doing father no good. After three or four days, I think, it was at the doctor's suggestion that the U. P. Government released Ranjit."

The released Congressmen were pouring into Allahabad. They were anxious to see the Great Man. A meeting of the Congress Working Committee was held at Swaraj Bhawan. The Nehrus were too much distraught to take any effective part in them. Most of them were in favour of the continuance of civil disobedience. Motilal could take no interest in the meetings. He was already far away from such happenings.

"I am going soon, Mahatmaji," he said to Gandhiji, "and I shall not be here to see Swaraj. But I know that you have won it and will soon have it."

Freshly out of prison the Congressmen were anxious to have a last glimpse of Motilal. These were farewell meetings. They came to him in twos and threes in the mornings and evenings. Father insisted on sitting up in an easy chair. He received his old comrades for the last time. There he sat massively and expressionlessly. The swelling of his face prevented much play of feeling. Friend followed friend. Comrade succeeded comrade. There was a glitter in the eyes of the lingering man. He recognised them all. Though he could not speak much, sometimes he did say a few words. His old humour did not leave him. There he sat like an old lion. He was mortally wounded. His physical strength was gone. But he was still very leonine and kingly. He was struggling with himself. He was trying to keep grip of things. It threatened to slip away from his grasp. To the end the struggle continued. He did not give in. Occasionally he spoke with extreme clarity. When he could not speak, he took to writing on slips.

Vijaya Lakshmi Pandit, Kamala, Krishna, Jawaharlal and mother hovered around father all the time. At night they took turns at his bedside in case he wanted anything. If he wanted anything, he asked for it very apologetically. He did not want to bother anybody. He was very considerate. Even in the throes of a fatal illness, his thought was for others. He never thought of himself. Day after day his children watched him anxiously. His strength ebbed away. But they were helpless. The house was full of guests. But only gloom pervaded everywhere. Silently people flitted about the house. The atmosphere was sorrowful. But Motilal did not lose heart.

"Often he joked with Gandhiji," says Krishna, "or teased mother about his going ahead of her and waiting to meet her in the next world, but never did he feel afraid of what he knew must be the inevitable end."

Motilal fought with death manfully. He fought with all his failing strength. He tried to live so that he might see the freedom of India. He desired that the meeting of the Working Committee should be held in Swaraj Bhawan. His last words were :

"Decide India's fate in Swaraj Bhawan ; decide it in my presence and let me be a party to the final honourable settlement of the fate of my motherland. Let me die, if die I must, in the lap of a free India. Let me sleep my last sleep not in a subject country, but in a free one."

The doctors decided to take him to Lucknow for X-Ray examination. Motilal did not like this. He knew that his death was at hand. And he did not want to leave his favourite home. But the doctors insisted. Gandhiji agreed. And the Great Man was too weak to protest. So he was taken to Lucknow by car. Even the long journey did not seem to strain his nerves. He seemed to be a bit better the next morning. But by the evening he was definitely worse. He could not breathe. Oxygen was given to him. He lay unconscious of everything. Three eminent doctors were attending upon him. Krishna, the younger daughter, gave him support at the eleventh hour. He kissed the girl as the last farewell. He mumbled with great difficulty :

" My daughter must be brave always."

No wonder the daughters of Motilal have come up to his expectations. Even at that time they faced the domestic and national calamity with calmness. Krishna clenched her teeth with superhuman effort. With superhuman effort she tried not to let her tears brim over.

Vijaya Lakshmi, Krishna, Kamala, and other attendants were worn out with fatigue. Towards the morning they fell asleep. Only Jawaharlal and his mother were present when the Great Man passed waay.

"Early next morning, February 6th," says Jawaharlal, "I was watching by his bedside. He had had a troublesome and restless night; suddenly I noticed that his face grew calm and the sense of struggle vanished from it. I thought that he had fallen asleep, and I was glad of it. But my mother's perceptions were keener, and she uttered a cry. I turned to her and begged her not to disturb him as he had fallen asleep. But that sleep was his last long sleep, and from it there was no awakening."

Vijaya Lakshmi and other girls filed into the room. Father lay on his bed as though asleep. His face was calm and peaceful. It was more majestic than it had been in his hife. The girls could not believe that their daddy was dead. Jawaharlal sat behind him. His hands were on father's head as though he was stroking it. His eyes were full of unshed tears. Then Gandhiji walked up to father's bed. He stood awhile with bent head. He was praying and bidding farewell to his comrade-in-arms. Then he went to Mrs. Motilal and said:

"Motilal is not dead; he will live long."

The news was flashed across the whole country. Hundreds and thousands of people flocked to the Kalakanker Palace where the Nehrus were staying. The people crowded to have the last darshan of their popular leader. The Great Man lay in state. His body was buried in flowers. An unending stream of visitors paid their last homage. Mrs. Motilal looked a forlorn and a pathetic figure. She had shared with him a lifetime of hardships and honours. Jawaharlal and Vijaya Lakshmi were worn-out and haggard. They seemed to have aged overnight. Outside the house the crowds were swelling. Grief was written on every face. No eye was dry. There was a hushed atmosphere.

Motilal was brought to Allahabad by car. His body was draped with the National Flag. Jawaharlal sat in the car and Ranjit S. Pandit had the honour of driving his father-in-law on his last journey. Hari, the favourite servant of the hero, was also in the car. Vijaya Lakshmi, Krishna, and Kamala drove ahead in order to reach home earlier for necessary arrangements. Gandhiji and Mrs. Motilal followed the hero in another car. The last car was delayed as they had an accident. It was Pandit Motilal Nehru's own car. As his chauffeur was crying, he did not see a big ditch in the middle of the road. So the car was upturned and the occupants—Gandhiji and Mrs. Motilal—had a miraculous escape.

After ceremonies at home, the Great Man was taken to the banks of the Ganges in a huge procession. The national flags were flown half-mast throughout the country. A mighty murmur went up from hundreds of throats. The bier was gorgeously decorated with flowers. Allahabad had never before witnessed such a procession. On the banks of the Ganges it was only a sea of bare heads waiting in silence. After the ceremonies, Gandhiji and Pandit Malaviya addressed the mourners. Gandhiji said :

"Let every man and woman bow here before the last remains of our great hero on the banks of Jumna and Ganges, that he or she will not rest till the freedom of India is achieved, because this was the great cause dear to the heart of Motilalji. It was this for which he gave his life."

The whole nation went into mourning. Hartals were held in every city. Schools and colleges were closed. All business was at a standstill for two days. Messages of sympathy poured in from all over the world. In a message Gandhiji said :

"My position is worse than a widow's. A widow by a faithful life can appropriate the merits of her husband. I can appropriate nothing. What I have lost through Motilaiji's death, is a loss for ever."

IV

INDIA MARCHED ON

When Motilal passed away, the India for which he had sacrificed himself, marched on.

"On the very day and almost at the very hour of my father's death," says Jawaharlal, "a large group of the Indian members of the Round Table Conference landed in Bombay."

Shortly after father's death, Jawaharlal left for Delhi. He was called thither by Gandhiji. The latter was having his talks with Lord Irwin. Out of them the Gandhi-Irwin Pact was hatched. But now Jawaharlal was the head of the little family and he did not forget Vijaya Lakshmi and other beloved members at home. In a letter to Krishna, Jawaharlal wrote:

"We are the children of our father and have something of his great strength and courage, and whatever the trials and difficulties that may come our way, we shall face them with resolution and with the determination to overcome them."

Vijaya Lakshmi felt the loss of her father very deeply. This sorrow was shared by all members of the family with the same intensity. The children felt so utterly lost without him. They did not know how to set about things. The pillar had fallen about their heads. Vijaya Lakshmi and Krishna showed the courage which their father had expected from of his daughters. Jawaharlal was like a balm to his sisters. He gave them courage to face life's problems.

The next session of the Indian National Congress was held at Karachi. Sardar Patel was the president. Mrs. Motilal, Krishna, Jawaharlal and his wife attended the session. Mrs. Vijaya Lakshmi Pandit did not go. Jawaharlal was not feeling well. So Jawaharlal, Kamala and Indira went to Ceylon.

The Gandhi-Irwin Pact did not improve the situation in the country. It was only a smoke-screen. The Government was not in a mood to accept the spirit of the pact. The fruits of the people's struggle were being thrown away. In the United Provinces there continued to be unrest. The peasants were on the march. And there was a deep-seated dissatisfaction among them. Ordinances were promulgated by the Government to suppress the mass movement. The Provincial Conference was banned. Gandhiji was returning from the Second Round Table Conference. And the Provincial Conference was postponed to meet him. But the U. P. leaders were not allowed to meet Gandhiji, because they were arrested as soon as he landed in Bombay.

Jawaharlal was arrested on way to Gandhiji. Two days later Gandhiji arrived in Bombay. He had expected to meet Jawaharlal at Ballard Pier. But there was no Jawaharlal to receive him. He was already behind the British bars.

The British wanted a fight. There was no alternative for the nationalists but to fight. The die was cast. And there was no turning back. Once again the battle began. Gandhiji and Sardar Patel were arrested without trial. The movement soon reached its zenith. The Congress workers threw themselves into the struggle. And the Nehrus found themselves in the thick of the battle. Undaunted by the domestic calamity, the Nehru girls, Lakshmi, Krishna and Kamala, were overwhelmed by enthusiasm. Even Mrs. Motilal Nehru did not lag behind. Aged and delicate though she was, she worked in the memory of her dear husband. She could not pass calmly over a cause for which Motilal Nehru had laid down his life. She went about addressing meetings like the Nehru girls from place to place.

V

PRISON DAYS

Vijaya Lakshmi was the first to be served with a notice. Soon it was repeated to Krishna and Kamala. They were ordered to refrain from taking part in meetings, processions and hartals. Independence Day was two weeks ahead. So the Nehru Girls decided to sleep over the political bed until then. On the Independence Day the Nehru Girls organised one of the largest meetings ever held in Allahabad. It was presided over by their mother. She made a fiery speech. There was a lathi charge and the meeting had to break up. Many were arrested on the spot. And a great many were injured. Although the Nehru Girls expected to be arrested, nothing happened. And they went home rather disappointed.

Vijaya Lakshmi and Krishna were informed next morning that they were under arrest. A police car arrived at nine o'clock. An Inspector of Police brought the warrant. Krishna thus describes her emotions :

" We got our things together and said goodbye to mother and others and then left for our prison home. It was our first real experience. I had been to jail once before for twelve hours. We had no thought for ourselves or our future, only for our frail little mother whom we had left behind all alone in the huge house which had known so much of joy and happiness, but knew only sorrow and loneliness now. It must have been very hard for mother to watch her children all go to jail, one by one leaving her alone to carry on her work as well as theirs. But though her body was frail, her heart was as proud and strong as that of a lioness and though she was left terribly alone with just her sister, another brave old lady, never once did she falter in her resolve to carry on the fight."

Thus Vijaya Lakshmi and Krishna drove away from their loved home to their new cell. When they reached there, many women comrades were already there. All were cheerful and smiling. They were prepared for anything that may befall them. They were glad to be together. They were weighed before they were taken inside. The prison had no special women's quarters. They were kept there only pending trials. And then they were transferred. Only one yard was kept for them. And in it were women of the worst type. They had all sorts of diseases. Amongst them were kept Vijaya Lakshmi and Krishna. There they stayed for three weeks before their trial. And four days after the trial they stayed there too. But the political prisoners were kept in separate cells. There were four women in every cell.

Each morning the Superintendent came on his rounds. He was an Englishman, shell-shocked during the last war. All women had to be present for him. He wanted to see with his own eyes that none was missing. One day the Nehru girls were rather late in appearing outside their cell. So the jailor got excited.

" Hurry up, hurry up," he said, " I can't wait here all day for you. I have to go to see the tennis tournament today and I am held up here in this most unpleasant place."

Nehru girls were very much annoyed. So Krishna retorted back:

" We find this even more annoying than you do as everything is so filthy here. And as you are missing your tournament, why should you not miss it one day when we are missing it daily?"

Their cells had all sorts of insects crawling around. For several nights they could not sleep. They were afraid if these dirty things get into their beds Some queer slimy insects might crawl up their arms or feet. It was an awful feeling. Once or twice it happened to all of them. Then they had a general clean-up before retiring at night. They were allowed visitors daily. And mother came to see them everyday.

Then the morning of their trial dawned. They waited for the appointed hour excitedly. The girls expected to get about six months. And they were quite prepared for the sentence. The trial took place in the jail. All the girls sat in a line. They were merely mentioned by name as each case was taken up. They refused to take part in the trial.

Vijaya Lakshmi was the first to be named. She did not offer any defence. The prosecution charge was produced. And Vijaya Lakshmi was sentenced to one year's rigorous imprisonment. And a fine was added to it. This harsh punishment took the women aback. But all of them were unperturbed. And Vijaya Lakshmi took everything as a matter of course. Krishna got the same sentence but without fine. Only two other girls got a year. Most of the women got only three to nine months. After four days they were transferred to Lucknow. Their departure took place at midnight. And in the Lucknow Prison, Vijaya Lakshmi and Krishna remained for eleven months and a half. They got a fortnight for good conduct.

The Nehru sisters arrived at Lucknow on a very cold winter morning. The grim prison walls towered above them sinister and unrelenting. It sank their hearts a little. For the first time they realized what prison life means. They were shut out from the outside world for a whole year. But the rigours did not cow down any one of the girls. They underwent all the hardships manfully. And they held fast to their faith in the cause of their country. A matron supervised their activities. They were free to walk about. But they were locked up at five o'clock in the evening. The hardened criminals looked at them sullenly. The wardress was a vindictive old hag. And she looked down upon them with great disdain.

The prisoners had their parade days on Mondays. The Superintendent came on inspection. Therefore, there was a great commotion from early in the morning. There was cleaning of the yards and barracks. Then all the convicts were lined up in very clean looking uniforms. They had their brightly-polished plates before them.

"Our Matron," says Krishna, "was rather perturbed on the first parade day, as she was not sure how we would behave when the seperintendent came to our barrack. All prisoners were supposed to stand up when he arrived, but in some jails the politicals had refused to do so and hence our Matron's concern."

Krishna, the younger sister, always took the initiative over Vijaya Lakshmi. It was the former who seems to have done most of the talking with the authorities. The first inspection passed off very peacefully, because the Superintendent was very courteous. He asked for comp'aints and requirements. So Krishna asked for some French and Italian books, some books on shorthand, some novels, and three dictionaries. It was a huge demand for a prisoner. The Superintendent hesitated.

"Would it not be better," he asked, "if I asked permission from the authorities to install a small library for you inside the jail? You would have a greater variety to pick and choose from."

"That would be lovely," said Krishna, "if it is not too much trouble to you. You see I do not want to waste my time here just twisting yarn. So I hope you will let me have the books soon."

The Government allowed the books after two months of hard deliberation. The girls were allowed six saries each and a few other garments. These they had to wash themselves everyday. And it was no easy task. The Khadi was thick and heavy. Soaked in water, it became even heavier. And it was very difficult to handle the washing. But they soon got used to many things in jail.

"The food we were given," says Krishna, "was terrible and though we made valiant efforts to eat it, we could not do so. It was not only that the food was bad that upset us. It was served up in such a dirty manner that it made one sick at the sight of it. We asked for permission to cook ourselves and this was granted. We made up batches of fours and sixes. One person in each group did the cooking, one cut the vegetables and others washed the dishes, etc. After this arrangement we felt a little happier."

There were ten or twelve persons in a barrack. All day they were free to roam around our yard. At five in the evening they were locked up and opened at six in the morning. These herd like hours were the most difficult to pass. At times they got on each other's nerves. On the whole they got on each other's patience. But on the whole they lived on merrily. News from outside were often disturbing. Once their mother was hurt in a lathi charge.

"Not having any particulars," says Krishna, "my sister and I were almost frantic with worry, and yet we were not allowed to send a telegram or a letter as we had both written our fortnightly letters some days ago. It was at such times that one felt helpless, bitter and frustrated."

Most of the Nehrus were already in jail. Only mother was out. She had to interview Jawaharlal, Ranjit S. Pandit, Vijiaya Lakshmi and Krishna. If she were ill, they had to forego their interview. And this was the most depressing for the Nehrus.

Every fortnight they were weighed. If they gained a pound or two, they blamed the scales. The ladies plagued the doctor fairly well.

" The Superintendent and the doctor," says Krishna, " were the only two men allowed in the women's prison and though the most ardent feminists among us denied emphatically that it was good to see a man occasionally, they spent most of the time he was in the yard talking to him and blaming him for everything that went wrong in jail."

Thus the life dragged on in the prisoners-of-war camp. Sometimes the sisters were dull and sad. At times they were happy and contented. They spent their time in reading and discussing. They found all the young girl convicts quite friendly. Some of them were amusing and clever. They could dance and sing. One of them was quite an expert at it. She was an Anglo-Indian girl and must have been very attractive in her youth. She was kept in a solitary cell, because she was ever getting into mischief.

The treatment meted out to young girl convicts made Nehru Girls very furious. The wardresses were of the worst type, but they could do nothing about it. The wardresses were rude and insulting to all the politicals. When they spoke, it was difficult for Nehru Girls to keep their temper.

They had to face the bitter winter nights without adequate shelter. There were no doors. And iron bars could not check the bitter winds. The spring ended all too soon. The summer set in with its dust storms and hot winds. Summer was even worse than winter. But the girls survived. Then there came the welcome rains.

"Towards the end of December," says Krishna, "my sister and I were released. Some of our comrades had left before us, others had come after us and we had to leave them behind. Even though we looked forward to going home again, we felt a little sad at deserting them."

Jail life was a good education for Vijaya Lakshmi and Krishna. They were glad to make friends with many of the convicts who are considered a menace to society. They were "far better specimens of humanity than many of the people we come across in our daily life." Nehru girls were glad to return home but it hurt them to know that these poor creatures would be left behind for many long long years. Most of these girls were sensitive, affectionate and understanding. And yet they were condemned to long terms of imprisonment.

The Nehru girls were not released in Lucknow. They were brought back to Allahabad by the Matron. When Vijaya Lakshmi and Krishna returned home, they found it completely deserted. Kamala was ill at Calcutta. And Anand Bhawan was locked up. No one knew of their release. But the news spread like wildfire. Within a couple of hours their house was full of friends. After the quiet jail life, this was rather overpowering. And the Nehru sisters were dazed.

VI

HEROINES AT HOME

Vijaya Lakshmi and Krishna went to Calcutta to meet Kamala and mother. When Kamala recovered, they all returned to Allahabad.

Vijaya Lakshmi, just before her arrest, had sent her three little daughters to a boarding school in Poona. The youngest was only three years old. Not having seen her children since a long time, Lakshmi was eager to go and meet them. The school belonged to some friends. Indira was also a boarder there. So Lakshmi and Krishna left for Bombay and Poona. They first went to Poona and then took the children on a trip to Bombay. In Poona they had several interviews with Gandhiji at Yervada. He always greeted them with great affection. And it did the girls some good to spend sometime with him.

Vijaya Lakshmi, Krishna, and the children were in Bombay for about a week. It was during this trip that Krishna met her would-be husband—Gunottam Hutheesingh. It was at a party. As soon as she entered the room, she noticed him. He looked somewhat different from all the others. There was a detached and rather superior air about him. It both annoyed and intrigued Krishna. Though one of the party, he seemed not to be of it. Apart from their introduction they did not speak at all.

"I usually notice," says Krishna, "people's hands when I meet them for the first time, for, to me they always seem to speak and to give an inkling into the person's character. So one of the first things I noticed about Raja were his hands : sensitive and artistic—they seemed to speak volumes for their owner who was exceptionally quiet."

In May Vijaya Lakshmi and Krishna went to Mussorrie. There they stayed for a couple of months. On return they decided to go to Ahmedabad. There she met Raja again. The only person whom Krishna mentioned her lover was Vijaya Lakshmi. On her return from Ahmedabad she told her that she wanted to marry him. She told her not to say anything about it to mother. Thus they kept the secret between

A YOUTHFUL FACE

which mocks at the dash of silver in the hair. Greyness is her hereditary weakness.

THE HEROINE RETURNS HOME

A right royal welcome was accorded to Mrs. Vijaya Lakshmi Pandit, India's great ambassador to U.S.A., on her return to India after a lecture tour of nearly thirteen months.

SHE STANDS STRAIGHT

hoping for the best, preparing for the worst, and leaving the rest to God.

SOLDIER OF SATYAGRAHA

Lakshmi is a typical member of Mahatma Gandhi's armless but indefatigable army.

themselves. When the mother recovered, Krishna requested Lakshmi to tell Jawaharlal about Raja.

The matter was kept a close secret during the illness of mother, but suitable time was discovered for domestic publicity.

" It was then," says Krishna, " that I asked Swarup to tell Jawahar about it. It did not seem unnatural to me to have chosen my future husband without consulting my people as I had always had freedom to do as I pleased. I did not dream of defying or going contrary to the wishes of my mother, brother or sister ; but I knew that they would not be unreasonable unless there was a very good reason for it. They knew nothing at all about Raja, but I was sure that they would not withold their consent, for my happiness came first with them, and I was only afraid they would think we had not known each other long enough which was true. But I did not think long engagements helped one to get to know each other any better."

Jawaharlal went to Bombay and met Raja. Then he met Gandhiji and told him the whole matter. Gandhiji had known the family of Raja and he gave his blessings to the couple. On October 20, 1933, they got married at Anand Bhawan according to Civil Marriage rites. The mothers of the couple were lying ill at that time at Allahabad and Ahmedabad, respectively. So it was a very brief wedding. Only the near relations of both the families were present. Lakshmi as well as Krishna was married with the approval of Gandhiji. In fact in the case of the former, Gandhiji's secretary had played a diplomatic part. Gandhiji wrote the following letter to Krishna :

" My dear Krishna. You are now going to be reborn, for marriage is a sort of rebirth, is it not? Your sister Swarup came as a bride to Kathiawar but persuaded her husband to go and settle down in her old Province. But there is a great deal of difference between Swarup and you, and I do not think you will try to take Raja away. Besides, Raja is a Gujarati who will not easily leave his homeland. So, I hope, you will make Gujarat your home, or may be Bombay. My only wish is that wherever you are, may you be happy and add lustre to the already bright name of your illustrious parents.

"I regret very much I am unable to attend your marriage, so I shall have to content myself with sending you my blessings.—Your Bapu."

It is clear from this letter the profound interest exhibited by Gandhiji in the welfare of Krishna and Vijaya Lakshmi. The contrast between the two sisters is indeed remarkable and nobody has failed to notice this. Sarojini Naidu also sent her congratulations in which she wrote:

"I see that Swarup and Kamala are here to get together a hurried trousseau for you, and are complaining of the limited choice that *shudh* (pure) Khadi offers for raiment. But why should that bother you, who move clothed in delight and dreams and are adorned with the jewels of your own youth and romance and adventure".

The following note about G. P. Hutheesingh (Raja), the husband of Krishna, and brother-in-law of Vijaya Lakshmi, appeared in the newspapers recently:

"Gunottam P. Hutheesingh, brother-in-law of Jawaharlal Nehru, has a right to have 'pride in his port and defiance in his eye,' though as a matter of fact I know him to be the most charming and mild-mannered of the youths who have made their mark recently in the politics of Western India. He traces his ancestry to a formidable great-great-grandfather, whose one job throughout life was to fight the British on every possible occasion. It was not his fault that the British won in the end. Till the last day he would not submit to their authority. He made a bid for immortality by building a Jain temple in Ahmedabad, known as the Hutheesing Temple. It is one of the outstanding architectural monuments of the city, beautiful in its design and pious in its execution.

" Gunottam's allegiance to the Congress began as early as 1920 when he left a local Government school and went to the Gujarati Vidyapith and matriculated from there. In 1926 he went to England and graduated from Oxford University. He put finishing touches to his foreign education by his studies at Heidelberg, Berlin and Paris (Sorbonne).

" In England he took an active part in student politics and counted among his contemporaries Sajjad Zaheer, Mahmud-uzzafar Khan, Iftikharuddin, ex-President of the Punjab Provincial Congress Committee.

" Returning to India in 1932, he was called to the bar. But politics continued to be his main attraction. He rejoined the Congress and after a couple of years was elected to the Bombay Provincial Congress Committee. His work as secretary of the China Ambulance Committee, of the Spanish Aid Committee and of the National Planning Committee is well-known."

The marriage of Krishna completed the disintegration of the Nehrus.

" Living as we did at Anand Bhawan," says Krishna, " my parents, Jawahar and his family, my sister and I, we made up this unit. But there never were any hard and fast rules by which any of us were tied down to the rest. We lived together in one house but led our individual lives, rarely if ever clashing with one another. No bonds held us together except bonds of affection which are stronger than anything else could be."

Wiser by the afflictions of Vijaya Lakshmi, his younger sister adopted a more domestic outlook of life.

"I knew only too well," says Krishna, "what politics meant, uncertainty, change, prison and long separations. I had had thirteen years of it and did not want to lose my newly acquired contentment and peacefulness. I did not wish to take active part in politics as my sons were very young. I had seen how Jawahar's and Swarup's children had suffered from infancy from having no family life, no settled home or routine."

That is true. Vijaya Lakshmi has never been able to pay adequate attention to her daughters. And if they have grown up to be sturdy nationalists, it is not because of her maternal care, but rather in spite of it.

In January 1935 Mrs. Motilal visited Bombay and there she had an attack of paralysis. She was terribly ill for a couple of months. Vijaya Lakshmi rushed to Bombay and there along with Krishna she nursed her. For days and nights she hovered between life and death. Therefore, they spent many anxious days and nights.

In April 1935, Kamala, the sister-in-law of Vijaya Lakshmi, fell seriously ill. The doctors suggested that she should go to Switzerland. Jawaharlal and Ranjit S. Pandit, the husband of Lakshmi, were in prison at that time. Another young man who kept them company for sometime was an outsider who got mixed up with Indian politics against the advice of Vijaya Lakshmi Pandit.

"A surprising addition to our little brotherhood of Barrack No. 6 was Bernard Aluvihare, a young friend from Ceylon, who had just returned from England after being called to the Bar. He had been told by my sister not to get mixed up with our demonstrations: but in a moment of enthusiasm, he joined a Congress Procession—and a Black Mark carried him to prison."

This was in Naini Prison. But Jawaharlal was in Almora Jail when his wife fell ill. Switzerland did not do Kamala much good. And therefore Jawaharlal had to be released. And he flew to Europe. Kamala died on February 28, 1936 in Switzerland. Her daughter Indira was by her side.

Jawaharlal was yet in Europe when he was elected President of the Indian National Congress. That year the session was held at Lucknow. He was re-elected next year for the Faizpur Congress. General elections were held throughout India. Provincial Autonomy was inaugurated. The Congress gained large majorities. Congress Cabinets were formed in the provinces.

Vijaya Lakshmi also became a Minister. She was the first and the only woman Minister in India.

CHAPTER SEVENTH

India's first Woman Minister

I am like a flag unfurled in space,
I scent the oncoming winds and must bend with them,
While things beneath are not yet stirring,
While the doors close gently and there is silence in the chimneys,
And the windows do not yet tremble and the dust is still heavy,
Yet I feel the storm and am vibrant like the sea,
And expand and withdraw into myself,
And thrust myself forth and am alone in the great storm.

—RAINER MARIA RILKE

(Translated from German by Jessie Lemont).

Vijaya Lakshmi unfurled her intellect like a tricolour in the political space of India. When she assumed the authority of a minister, she was the first woman, after the fall of Rani of Jhansi in 1857, who came to something like a temporary throne of a nominal ruling princess. That she is a Nehru is a great credit to the Nehru family, because the Nehrus have helped the people to regain what our rulers lost to the European imperialists. India's struggle against the British has been a bitter one, and in this struggle the Nehrus, men, women and children, have played a heroic part. When Motilal Nehru died, Jawaharlal filled the gap in Indian politics. And now Vijaya Lakshmi came forward to give lead to the fair sex of India.

I

THE INTERNATIONAL HORIZON

These were the uncertain days of burning international politics. Munich was a shock hard to bear for the freedom-fighters in India. The tragedy of Spain became a personal sorrow to many an Indian. Horror succeeded horror. The sense of impending catastrophe overwhelmed the globe. Our faith in the bright future for the world became dim. General Franco's rising had a background of Italian and German assistance. It was developing into world conflict. And India was being drawn to the whirlpool. The political problems of China, Abyssinia, Palestine and Spain, were facets of one and the same world problem which also drew India into the vortex.

" As peace was said to be indivisible in the present-day world," says Jawaharlal, "so also was freedom indivisible, and the world could not continue for long, part free and part unfree. The challenge of fascism and Nazism was in essence the challenge of imperialism. They were twin brothers, with this variation, that imperialism functioned abroad in colonies and dependencies, while fascism and Nazism functioned in the same way in the home country also. If freedom was to be established in the world not only fascism and Nazism had to go but imperialism had to be completely liquidated."

This feeling to foreign events was not confined to Jawaharlal. Vijaya Lakshmi reacted in the same way. Many other politicians in India felt likewise. Even the Indian public was interested in international politics. The Congress organised thousands of meetings and demonstrations all over the country in sympathy with the people of China, Abyssinia, Palestine and Spain. India sent medical supplies and food to Spain and China. This wider interest in international politics helped to raise India's national struggle to a higher level.

II

ELECTIONS IN INDIA

Foreign affairs did not touch the life of the average Indian. He was absorbed in his own troubles. The peasant was full of his growing difficulties. Many burdens crushed him. Appaling poverty stalked in the land of Hindustan. The agrarian problem was the major problem of India. The Congress evolved an agrarian programme. The industrial worker was as badly off as the peasant. A constitution was imposed upon India by the British Parliament. And it was being discussed by the politically-minded people.

" This constitution," says Jawaharlal, " though giving some power in the provinces, kept the reality of power in the hands of British Government and their representatives. For the Central Government a Federation was proposed which tied up feudal and autocratic states with semi-democratic provinces, and was intended to perpetuate the British imperialist structure. It was a fantastic affair which could never work, and which had every safeguard that the wit of man could devise to protect British interests. The Constitution was indignantly rejected by the Congress, and in fact there was hardly any one in India who had a good word for it."

Even though the Congress had rejected the Constitution, it decided to contest the elections. It was wise to determine the national will. The Congress wanted to fight the Constitution inside and outside the provincial legislatures, and thereby kill the federal scheme. Thus the Congress came to figure in the Provincial Autonomy.

Then came the General Elections of the year 1936. She stood up as a Congress candidate for the United Provinces

Legislative Assembly. It was from Cawnpore Bilhaur Rural Constituency. It consisted of about 38,000 men and women. Her opponent in the contest was lady Srivastava, the wife of the then Minister of Education. The country was pulsating with a new sense of patriotism. The congress was scoring victory after victory.

" Previous to that my knowledge of elections had been vague and corresponded somewhat to Hyde Park oratory," she said.

The actual election campaign in villages of the Cawnpore District was a new revelation to her. She toured throughout the length and breadth of the province with her workers by trains, by motor car or on bullock carts, and even on foot. Actual contact with the starving millions of India added to her information. It greatly enriched her knowledge of social and political affairs. The laborious task of election propaganda was another thrill in her bold and adventurous existence. She was asked to fight a difficult seat. Her rival in the election was the wife of the minister of education. But the very name of Congress was enough to inspire the voters. They voted for her. They enabled her to thwart anyone who ventured to oppose her. In one of her writings she narrates an interesting episode. Travelling in her constituency, she one day happened to enter a Railway compartment. It was already occupied by an Indian student and an American. There was a hot discussion going on between them. In the meanwhile the talk turned on to elections. They began to discuss the chances of her success. Neither the Indian student nor the American tourist recognised her. She therefore sat as an interested spectator. The American asked the Indian student what exactly she had done to deserve such admiration.

"Done!" the Indian student exclaimed in reply, "she does not have to do anything. She is our mother and sister and she will win."

This general election was a memorable affair. The topmost leaders were themselves not candidates. But they toured all over India on behalf of the Congress. Jawaharlal, the unique brother of Vijaya Lakshmi played a unique part.

"I created," he says, "some kind of a record in the way of election campaigns."

In the course of about four months, he travelled nearly fifty thousand miles. He used every kind of conveyance for this purpose. Often he went into remote rural areas. There were no proper means of transport.

"I travelled," he says, "by aeroplane, railway, automobile, motor lorry, horse carriages of various kinds, bullock cart, bicycle, elephant, camel, horse, steamer, paddle-boat, canoe, and foot."

Jawaharlal, the then Congress President, carried microphones and loudspeakers with him. He addressed dozen meetings a day. He spoke to impromptu gatherings by the roadside. Some mammoth gatherings approached a hundred thousands. Sometimes it was much greater. The average audience was usually twenty-thousand. On a rough estimate it can be said that ten million persons actually attended the meetings he addressed. He met several millions more during his journeyings.

The Election Commander rushed from place to place. Enormous enthusiasm met him. And he was kept by the excitement of the moment. An extraordinary feat of physical endurance surprised him. A new life was visible everywhere.

"For me it was a voyage of discovery of India and her people," says Jawaharlal. "I saw a thousand facets of this country of mine in all their rich diversity, and yet always with the unifying impress of India upon them. I gazed at the millions of friendly eyes that looked up at me and tried to understand what lay behind them. The more I saw of India, the more I felt how little I knew of her infinite charm and variety."

Congressites were applauded by the enthusiastic millions of the land. The Congress swept the polls. Vijaya Lakshmi Pandit won the Election by 1,000 votes.

The Election fever was over. One fine morning came a telegram from Pandit Govind Ballabh Pant. He requested Vijaya Lakshmi if she would join his cabinet as a Minister. She did not want to join the ministry, she had already vehemently opposed the proposal of office-acceptance moved by Sjt. C. Rajagopalachari in the Congress Working Committee. The advice of those whose opinion she valued led her to accept the job. As a member of the Congress she had been trained to obey orders from those placed above her. Besides in offering her a seat in the U. P. Cabinet, the Congress was advocating the principle of equality between the sexes.

III

LAKSHMI ENTERS THE CABINET

Vijaya Lakshmi's admission into the Cabinet was a matter of great satisfaction to her sister. It was a fitting honour to the Nehru family for their endless sacrifices. Motilal Nehru had stated that ladies could serve the country in politics even better than men. His prophecy was coming true. It was not merely his son who kept alive the great traditions of a great family. Now a great girl was holding aloft the good name of her father. Throughout the United Provinces no better person could have been found to shoulder the problems of health and sanitation than a member of the Anand Bhawan which was a model of good living in the province.

"From her childhood," says Krishna, "Swarup (Vijaya Lakshmi) had been a very tactful person and was eminently suited to become a Minister. She seldom if ever gets agitated over anything and deals with all kinds of situations in a calm unruffled manner. Charming, self-possessed and beautiful, she has little difficulty in winning people over. As a Minister she was a great success. It was a difficult task she undertook to perform, never having been trained for any work of that time, but she excelled herself at it and was very popular. When Swarup started taking an active part in politics her ability as a speaker surprised us all. She seemed to have been born to it and seldom showed any signs of nervousness, no matter how large the gathering which she had to address. She speaks with fluency and ease both in Hindustani and in English."

Is there any wonder that Pandit Pant offered her a Ministership? It was little favour done to her. She amply deserved it.

On Thursday, the 29th July, 1937 at 11 a.m. the United Provinces Assembly met at the Assembly hall, where Vijaya Lakshmi took her oath as the Minister for Local Self-Government.

Before that her knowledge of a Council in action was confined to a few occasions. As a girl she sat in the visitor's gallery in the Assembly Chamber in Dehli or Simla when her father led the Swaraj Party in the Assembly.

Soon after dawned the day when she was to make her maiden speech in the Assembly. She was not a novice at public speaking, she had many occasions of addressing public meetings. But she had never before spoken in the Assembly. The first Government resolution, rejecting the Government of India Act and demanding a new Act to be framed by a Constituent Assembly, representing the will of the Indian people, was to be moved by the Premier. He, however, was suddenly confined to bed. And the choice fell on Mrs. Vijaya Lakshmi Pandit. She courageously stood up. Casting off nervousness, she mustered up equipoise. And she began to speak. The speech went off smoothly. And her stage fright vanished. Every one has to pass through the initial stage of apprenticeship. And so she did. With a marvellous promptitude she picked up the technique of the Secretariat boss and the Legislator. Even the veterans of the time wondered at her ability. It was resolved :

"This Assembly is of opinion that the Government of India Act 1935, in no way represents the will of the Nation and is wholly unsatisfactory, as it has been designed to perpetuate the subjection of the people of India. The Assembly demands that this should be repealed and replaced by a constitution for a free India framed by a Constituent Assembly elected on the basis of adult franchise, which allows the Indian people full scope for development according to their needs and desires."

Whereupon Mr. Muhammad Ismail Khan stood up to move an amendment that the Constituent Assembly be convened "provided that in the absence of an agree' settlement the measure and the method of the representation of the Muslims to the Constituent Assembly shall be the same as that provided in the Communal Award and provided further that the Constituent Assembly shall not be competent to alter or vary the personal law on the existing civil, political and religious rights of the Muslims without the consent of three-fourths of the Muslim representation."

And Nawab Dr. Sir Muhammad Ahmad Said Khan hastened to safeguard the interests of landlords and capitalists. He added. "Provided that landlords, depressed classes and other minority communities, shall receive adequate and special representation and that the Constituent Assembly shall not interfere with lawful and legitimate rights and interests in private property."

IV

LAKSHMI AT HOME

If Lakshmi was an angel in politics, she was a drudge at home. It was not a mere fortune that brought her success. She had worked herself to death for India. While still quite young, her hair started greying. All too rapidly more and more silver entered into her golden hair. Now she has almost silvery white hair. But it enhances her beauty. Her loveliness is captivating.

"She is a capable mother," says Krishna, "and an efficient housewife. In spite of the fact that politics takes up a great deal of her time, she still finds time to look after her home and children."

One evening in 1938 found all the elder Nehrus together at Anand Bhawan in Allahabad. Vijaya Lakshmi, Jawaharlal and Krishna were there with their mother. It was a mere chance. But does anything ever happen in the world by chance? The husband of Vijaya Lakshmi and her children were also there Mother was feeling the brighter and stronger for the last few days. That evening she seemed quite vivacious.

All the Nehrus had their dinner together and they were in a reminiscent mood. Mother talked more than usual. And they were happy. After dinner they sat and chatted till late at night. Vijaya Lakshmi was due to go to Lucknow at midnight. Mother was not feeling sleepy. So she sat up till it was time for Vijaya Lakshmi to leave for the station. They tried to dissuade Lakshmi but she would not listen. So they sat and talked.

At eleven o'clock Lakshmi got ready to go. She went to mother to say goodbye. As mother rose to embrace Lakshmi, she suddenly crumpled up. She would have fallen down, but Jawaharlal and Krishna rushed to Lakshmi's assistance. They helped mother to bed. Even before they laid her down, she became unconscions. Mother had two attacks of paralysis before. This was the third. The doctor was sent for. But he shook his head. He said that there was no hope. She would die in a few hours. The young Nehrus had never known sudden death. And so they were stunned. Mother parted from her beloved children even without kissing them goodbye. All through the night they watched beside their mother's bed—Jawaharlal, Vijaya Lakshmi, Krishna, and their aunt Bibi Amma. At five in the morning her difficult breathing stopped. She lay quiet and at peace. The lovely adored mother of Vijaya Lakshmi had gone to sleep from which there was no awakening.

Bibi Amma was not in the room when Mrs. Motilal died. So Vijaya Lakshmi went to break the news to her. She was too stunned to believe. She considered it impossible that her younger sister should die so suddenly while she herself was alive. Gradually her mind grasped the tragic fact. Her courageous heart suffered a tremendous shock. Her heart bled. Her senses reeled. She hid her grief to lessen the grief of children. She made all the necessary arrangements for the funeral of her sister. With her own hands she got everything ready for the last rites. The funeral cortege left the house. And Bibi Amma stood in the verandah like a statue. She neither moved nor shed a single tear. She gazed at the flower-decked bier till she could gaze no more.

Quickly she turned away and walked back to her sister's room. She was looking as though for the last time on all things that had been dear to her sister. She had a stunned appearance. She lay down just where her sister used to lie.

"I lived for her," she said, "and now what is there to live for ? My task is done. I too must go."

When Jawaharlal and Vijaya Lakshmi returned from the funeral of their mother, they found that their aunt had a stroke the same as their mother. Vijaya Lakshmi was alarmed. And she sent for a doctor. The doctor was alarmed too. He declared that she was suffering from paralysis.

"We could hardly believe it," says Krishna, "for never in her life had she a stroke before nor had she ever been seriously ill."

She lay unconscious. There was nothing one could do to save her. Everyone was very upset. All they could do was to wait and watch. They passed another restless night as they had passed the previons night. It was as though their heart would crack into thousand agonised bits.

"All through the night," says Krishna, "we watched and at 5 a.m., the next morning, exactly twenty-four hours after mother's death, Bibi Amma passed away. It seemed impossible that our mother and aunt should both die within twenty-four hours of each other, leaving us utterly lost and desolate."

So another funeral took place before the eyes of Vijaya Lakshmi within twenty-four hours. Two funerals were different from one another. Bibi Amma was a Sanyasi and she had died at will. Therefore no funeral rites were performed. They dressed her in a saffron sari. She had no other ornaments but her beauty.

"Dying as she did a day after mother," says Krishna, "when to all appearance she was hale and hearty, made people look upon her as a saint, for who else could have given up her life in such a manner."

Thousands of people gathered together at the funeral of the two sisters. Lined and aged their faces suddenly became youthful. Wrinkles disappeared. Their faces showed peace. Their souls were happy and at rest. Like queens they were carried to the cremation grounds.

V

LAKSHMI IN OFFICE

"I had an exceedingly vague idea," she says, of "the duties of a Minister when on the 18th July, 1937, I entered my office room in the Civil Secretariat for the first time".

A youngman presented himself to her. He told her that he was her Personal Assistant. And she began to wonder as to what all that meant. The Personal Assistant was naturally well acquainted with the Secretariat practices. He wondered at her ignorance. In a charmingly innocent way she enquired from him if it was possible to remove some of the unwanted furniture from the office. She was told it was permissible. But it was the furniture of bureaucracy that she really desired to get rid of.

She lived a life full of struggle. Her career was begemmed with intervals of gloomy days of jail existence and rough political strifes. It is the lot of every political worker in India.

Nevertheless she has kept alive within her a flame for the delicacies and fineries of life. She has a highly developed sense of culture and an exquisitely sensitive eye for Beauty. The aesthetic soul within her refused to be petrified by the dullness and drudgery of the jail. The red-tape machine of the Secretariat did not wither the flower of her heart.

She stood in her office in the Secretariat. Pink carpet struck a discordent note against the apple-green distemper on the walls. She stood in the door-way. She surveyed the room with a sinking heart. The 'Artist' in her was wounded. The pink carpet was quickly removed. In place of that delightful bluish-green one was substituted. Angle of the table was changed. A couple of blue-green curtains were asked for from her home. Something still seemed lacking. Yes, flowers! She sent for a green bowl and ordered it to be fitted with roses from the Secretariat gardens.

A green-coloured carpet! curtains to match! and a bowlful of roses! All that was procured. But then there were big old and gloomy files on her table. Life is not all 'art' and surely none else would do that inartistic work for her. How on earth could she tackle the screws! Her marvellous quality was of taking things in a cheerful spirit. Adjusting herself proved a guardian angel. Her habit of plunging into a problem straightaway came in handy. She just took up a file. It looked less complicated than the rest. She began to read.

"Soon I was engrossed in it and by the time I had read it through, felt quite competent to pass an order."

She went on with greater confidence to the next file. And then to the next. By the afternoon she had learnt the proper method of going through Secretariat files. She was passing orders on them.

There came a giant, six feet in height. He was her Departmental Secretary. Good heavens! She managed that giant, short as she looked in stature. Men claim themselves to be superior to women. A woman who was brought up in the natural course of life imbibed all the characteristics of Indian womanhood. It should look a little embarrassing in a position where she was required to deal with a team of Personal Assistants. Her indomitable courage and the strong will to work came to her rescue. She managed her Secretaries and managed them well.

Immediately she came into the limelight as a Minister. And she had to undergo the ordeal. She humorously refers to journalists as a pest!

"It is my opinion that the two greatest pests in the world today are the telephone and the journalist. The telephone can, however, be disconnected......but the journalists cannot," she says.

"How is it you have accepted a seat in the Cabinet after your opposition to acceptance of office?" asked a journalist, and irrespective of the reply that she gave or wanted to give, next day the papers announced, "Mrs. Pandit yielded to accept Ministership........"

Again, speaking to girl students, she advised them not to be influenced by prejudiced ideas. They should resist the tyranny of customs wherever they crippled their personality. During the speech she made a passing reference to a letter on divorce published in a certain paper. And the next day her speech was captioned as "Mrs. Pandit supporting divorce for women."

Her experience in Europe was even more painful.

Asked a Journalist: "what do you think of physical culture?"

She replied, " Oh, yes, I am a believer in it specially the Indian variety."

And next day a popular daily announced " Woman Minister begins 18 hour day by standing on head !"

Another journalist entered. He asked her if her acquaintance with Mr. Pandit started in the jail, she told him that she had been ten years married before she went to jail. Next day a newspaper gave interesting details of her life. It cooked out a romantic meeting with Mr. Pandit in jail. Later on it led to their marriage.

During the gay hours of her Ministership, invitation cards piled one after the other on her table. She had an occasional glimpse of fairy lights in rosy gardens. She witnessed tennis tournaments. She attended parties. She enjoyed festivities. All that she watched as a passing pageant. Her mind heard, " Far away in the distance......the cry of the oppressed and the hungry—the cry which gains in strength and volume as hours go by."

It pained her much when she read about the " Rioting in Cawnpore," the " Agitation in Bandhel Khand " and the "Tyranny let loose on Rajkot state subjects." It depressed her all the more when she tried to discuss the news with educated people. They had not even cared to read them.

She was the head of the Local Self-Government Dept. covering Health and Sanitation. Up to the year 1914 the administration of Health and Sanitation Department was vested in a Sanitary Commissioner. After that the Public Health item was transferred to the Local bodies. It continued to be controlled by them without any help, supervision or guidance, from the Provincial Government. In 1927, the Government commenced recruiting officers in the Provincial Medical Service. The work of the local health and sanitation "went forward with impetuous speed."

Her oratory burst forth cool and convincing. Her enthusiasm knew no bounds when she was sometimes required to speak on her favourite topic. It was the social condition of women in India. What astonished her rivals was her presence of mind, and the brilliancy of wit. She maintained them in her speeches even while speaking to and replying the questions of distinguished elder legislators of the province. In March 1938 she was one day on the floor of the house making some reference to Indian womanhood of the day. Thereupon Mr. H. G. Walford intervened and shot forth an interrogation:

"Are not the women of this country depressed and suppressed?"

And presently she admitted "Mr. Walford has rightly said that women are depressed and suppressed."

"I say that they are oppressed also," she added in a loud emotional tone, which added emphasis and charm to her expression.

Mr. H. G. Walford had, however, unnecessarily interrupted and made an uncalled for remark which attacked Indian womanhood. She therefore would not let the questioner and other members of his sex go unremonstrated. With added vigour therefore she continued:

"And since I have this opportunity I would like to request some of the honourable members who have made such chivalrous and beautifully high-sounding speeches about women to try and come forward and translate all this beauty of their words into the beauty of action."

There was pin-drop silence in the house and members, all attention, listened to the subdued remonstration of a courageous woman.

She explained to the house the policy of the Congress Ministry in respect of public health. Once addressing the Members in Hindustani, she said :

" The Government desire that in every village and every district there should be adequate arrangement to safeguard public health. Every one should get satisfactory medical aid...... the present rate of infant mortality should be checked. We wish to do all this and we will do all this."

Referring to untouchability she once remarked. ' It is some times asked what has the Congress Ministry done for the Achuts (Untouchables). The Honourable members perhaps do not know that in the Congress there is no Achut. The very word, which is repugnant to humanity, is not to be found in the Congress dictionary."

When Vijaya Lakshmi Pandit took charge of the Department, she had many problems to solve, many obstacles to overcome, and many miracles to perform.

In some rural areas drinking water facilities did not exist. Inhabitants of those places were rather hard pressed for pure drinking water. Maternity and child-welfare facilities were almost non-existent. Arrangements regarding public health were very poor. There was no sanitation in the villages scattered far away from the centres of modern life. It was very hard for the villager to get medical relief. He had to walk many miles to get the services of a doctor. The Government did not afford to open one hospital in each village. They thought it was rather a costly enterprise. This task, was impossible for the bureaucracy to accomplish. They blamed the natural antipathy of the ignorant masses against the allopathic treatment. The people would rather go to a Hakim than a doctor, was a lame excuse.

Notwithstanding on one hand the prejudices of the official folk and on the contrary the financial stringency in the budget for the year 1938-39, she presented a scheme to the house proposing 300 dispensaries in the rural areas. Out of this 200 dispensaries were to be under charge of Indian practitioners of indigenous system of medicine and 100 dispensaries under allopathic doctors. Some ultra-modern members of the house criticized the indigenous system. Convinced as she was that Ayurveda and Unani systems of treatment have their merits, she stuck to her guns and carried the enemy batteries before her.

Provision of maternity facilities was yet another task. The Indian Red Cross Society was carrying on the work of training ladies, mostly Christians, for others would not come forth for the profession, with a view to turn out midwives and nurses. The Red Cross Society was aided by the Government. The experiment however, did not succeed. The failure of the experiment was not due to lack of zeal on her part. The prejudices of the ignorant people, stood in her way. In a statement in the Assembly, she said :

" I regret to have to admit that these midwives are not at all popular, and in spite of the fact that the Red Cross Society has turned out more midwives now who are slightly better trained and of a better social standing, still they are looked down upon with suspicion and even where these Dais are available, the women of that part prefer not to make use of their services.

" People must be convinced that the work of a midwife is not a work to be looked down upon, and done by the very lowest in the land but that it is honourable work. This sort of thing can only be done by propaganda."

Apart from the activities of the Indian Red Cross Society, the Medical School for women at Agra was converted in.o a nursing Centre from the 1st January, 1939. The supply of these nurses to the Hospitals improved the prospects of Public Health.

Under her guidance a masterly Anti-malarial Scheme was prepared. The Ministry intended to spend about Rs. 80,000 with a view to combat malaria where it was prevalent in the most pernicious form.

In some villages where drinking water facilities did not exist, Rs. 35,000 were provided for the construction of wells.

She laid great stress on the opening of playgrounds for open-air exercise in villages and towns. In 1938-39 some 45,000 rupees were sanctioned for 48 districts. The District and Municipal Boards were also requested to provide play-grounds and Akharas for the benefit of children and adults. 175 play-grounds were opened in rural places and 10 in the Municipal areas.

Out of the funds sanctioned for medical aid in rural areas in 1938-39 budget, 16 travelling dispensaries, 48 fixed dispensaries, 24 maternity and child-welfare centres and 192 Aushadhalayas and Davakhanas were established.

Next year health schemes were extended to five more districts. Four new anti-rabic centres were opened. Maternity and child-welfare centres were stablized. Drinking water wells were improved upon.

She had milk scheme for children of the Province. The idea was to supply every child in Municipal and Urban areas with a certain quantity of milk every evening after they had done physical exercises in the newly constructed play grounds in both rural and urban areas. The scheme, however, had to be postponed due to financial stringency. The experiment was tried only in Agra District, with some success.

Duting her public activities she made a special effort to convert night schools into real adult literacy Centres. She strove to model evening institutions on Russian principles of Education. She adopted them to suit Indian conditions.

It was monetary stringency which the Ministry faced. She could not succeed in maturing schemes of Public hygiene, Maternity and Child Welfare. These would prove most beneficial to the people. Whatever little bits of funds she had at her disposal, she utilized them most scrupulously for the public welfare.

" We do not wish to spend a single pie of tax-payers money without fullest consideration," she declared.

Then came the war and the Civil Disobedience Movement when she with other Ministers resigned her job.

VI

CONGRESS CABINETS AT WORK

New problems faced India. In most of the provinces Congress Governments were at work. Many of the Ministers had spent years in prison.

" My sister, Vijaya Lakshmi Pandit," says Jawaharlal with righteous pride, " became one of the Ministers in the United Provinces—the first woman Minister in India."

The coming-in-power of Congress Ministries created a sense of relief in the countryside. A new life coursed through the whole country. The peasant and the worker expected big things to happen. Political prisoners were released. A large measure of civil liberty was established.

"The Congress Ministers worked hard," says Jawaharlal, "and they made others work hard also."

But the Congress cabinets had to work with the old apparatus of Government. It was wholly alien to them and very often it was hostile. Even the services were not under their control. Twice there was a conflict with the governors. And the ministers offered their resignations. Thereupon the Governors accepted the viewpoint of the ministers. And the crisis ended.

"But the power and influence of the old services—the Civil Service, Police, and others," says Jawaharlal, "backed by the Governor and buttressed by the Constitution itself, were great and could make themselves felt in a hundred ways."

Progress was slow. And dissatisfaction arose. This dissatisfaction found expression in the Congress. The more advanced elements grew restive. The fine fighting organisation was lying idle. A struggle for independence seemed inevitable. The phase of Provincial Autonomy was a passing one. Jawaharlal was hard on the Congress Ministers. He wrote to Gandhiji :

"They are trying to adapt themselves far too much to the old order and trying to justify it. But all this bad as it is might be tolerated. What is far worse is that we are losing the high position that we have built up, with so much labour, in the hearts of the people. We are sinking to the level of ordinary politicians."

The fault lay in the situation and the circumstances. It is clear from the activities of Vijaya Lakshmi that the record of the Congress Ministers was a formidable one. They had to work within certain limits. The national problems required the breaking down of such hedge-walls. Nevertheless they did many good things. They passed certain agrarian measures. And these gave considerable relief to the peasant. They made Basic Eduction free and compulsory for all. The system is full of promise. Higher reduction was also tackled vigorously. Public Health was also looked after, and in U. P. it was in the charge of Vijaya Lakshmi. Adult literacy was pushed with enthusiasm. And it yielded good results. Rural Reconstruction also came in for good deal of attention. Thus the record of the Congress Ministries was quite impressive.

The national interests required the ending of the imperialistic disease. So conflict grew within the Congress. The more advanced sections, opposed the more moderate elements. This distressed the Working Committee greatly. Subhas Bose was elected president of the next Congress Session. The world was on the edge of a great upheaval—Second World War. The situation in Europe in August 1939 was threatening. The War broke out.

What was the Congress to do ? Their aim was to struggle for India's independence, and not to enjoy cosy jobs ? The Congressmen were ready to face the ordeal with courage.

" The British Government," says Jawaharlal, " declared India to be a belligerant country without any reference to our people, to the Central Assembly, or to the Provincial Governments. That was a slight hard to get over, for it signified that imperialism functioned as before. The Congress Working Committee issued a long statement in the middle of September 1939, in which our past and present policy was defined and the British Government was invited to explain their war aims, more particularly with regard to British Imperialism. We had frequently condemned Fascism and Nazism but we were more intimately concerned with the imperialism that dominated over us. Was this imperialism to go ? "

which is being fought many thousands of miles away from here. Our opinion and advice has not heen sought, because being an enslaved nation of what value is our opinion or our advice. We are informed that this war that is being fought is a war of righteousness, that this is being fought for those principles which go to make life worth living whether for the individual or for the nation. But these brave words have ceased to have any meaning for us because throughout the centuries Britain has prefaced all declarations of war in a similar manner. It is, therefore, our right to know where we stand. It is our right to demand from Britain what the better world order is which we are to create... "

She requested different communities of India to unite and capture power from Britain. She said :

" Let us put our heads together and evolve a better method of democratic procedure...We have enough experience of empty promises in the past. Let us not fall into this trap again, for years and years the British policy has been to magnify our differences, seeing divergence of policies where merely differences of temperament exist.

" Let us now give a challenge to Britain that the people of India stand united and if our co-operation is of any value to Britain, it can be conceded as a free nation and an equal partner. If our just demand is rejected, the war degenerates into a war between two Imperialistic powers, for world demonation. The interest of our country demands our unity in face of a common and growing danger. Let us not hold back, because remember—If India dies who lives ? If India lives, who dies ? "

Many useful Bills were introduced by her in the Legislative Assembly such as the United Provinces Municipalities Amendment Bill (1939), and the United Provinces District Boards Amendment Bill, (1939). These proposed to transfer the control of Education to District Boards with a view to expedite educational progress in the province. The United Provinces Indian Medicine Bill was passed in 1939. Thus she was in the thick of her public activities when she had to resign and bid goodbye to the ministerial chair.

VIII

THE WAR WORE ON

As the war progressed, new problems arose. The old problems took a new shape. The old alignments seemed to change. The old standards faded away. There were many shocks. Adjustments were not easy. Russo-German Pact was a great surprise. Sheer opportunism ruled the world. Paris, the nursery of freedom, lay crushed and fallen.

"Not only military defeat came to France," says Jawaharlal, "but, what was infinitely worse, spiritual submission and degradation."

There was something rotten at the core of Europe. England and France represented an old order that must pass. They could not fight for their freedom because they denied it to others. Imperialism was turning to unabashed Fascism. In India there was no hint to change. England had lost capacity for anything effective. The lack of vision in the British Government was amazing. They utterly failed to read the signs of the times. The British system had failed to have any useful function.

"If the British Government was slow of understanding and could not even learn from experience," says Nehru, "what can one say about the Government of India?

There is something comic and something tragic about this Government, for nothing seems to shake it out of its age-long complacency; neither logic nor reason, neither peril nor disaster. Like Rip Van Winkle they sleep, even though waking, on Simla hill."

Mahatma Gandhi started Individual Satyagraha Movement so as to permit only chosen people to undertake it. It was intended as a token of Civil Disobedience, because Gandhiji did not want to embarras the Government. Vijaya Lakshmi offerred her services. And her services were accepted.

On December 9th, 1940, she was arrested as a satyagrahi in the Non-Violent Campaign. She was sentenced to 4 months' simple imprisonment. She spent the full term of sentence in Naini Central Jail.

Many persons submitted their names to Gandhiji for Satyagraha, but very few got the opportunity. Consequently, if Vijaya Lakshmi Pandit was enlisted by the Mahatma, it is because he included her in the golden record of most selected disciples of his. But Individual Satyagraha did not create much enthusiasm in the country. And also it did not harm the bureaucracy in any way. It was only a pin-pricking. And it did not tingle the skin of the British lion very much. At last the Satyagraha was called off by the Mahatma. And in this way ended an important experiment of Gandhiji.

Gandhiji wanted the Congress to extend the principle of non-violence to the functioning of a free state. As a matter of fact, there was nothing new in it, because Asoka had practised it quite successfully in the past. Gandhiji wanted the Congress to rely on this principle to guard itself against foreign aggression. The problem occupied his own mind. And he felt that the time had come for clear enunciation.

"'Every one of us was convinced," says Nehru, "that we must adhere to our policy of non-violence, as we had so far done, in our struggle. The war in Europe had strengthened this conviction. But to commit the future state was another and a more difficult matter, and it was not easy to see how anyone moving on the plane of politics could do it. Mr. Gandhi felt, and probably rightly, that he could not give up or tone down a message which he had for the world. He must have freedom to give it as he liked and must not be kept back by political exigencies. So for the first time, he went one way and the Congress Working Committee another."

While Vijaya Lakshmi Pandit was enjoying a brief respite behind the bars, the struggle for freedom was disentangling itself through the complicated uncertainties of the War, and new forces were shaping themselves. Yet the personality of Gandhiji towered over all. He has been the architect of India's destiny for two decades. And he was still working ceaselessly in the walls of time.

Rajagopalachari made another offer to the British Government on behalf of the Congress. He was eager to avoid a conflict between India and Britain during War. His proposal was hesitatingly accepted by his colleagues in the Congress. The proposal was the immediate formation of the Provisional National Government at the Centre which should be responsible to the present Legislative Assembly. In case this was done, the Congress agreed to help the war effort of the Government even against the wishes of Gandhiji.

The Congress plan was immensely practicable. And it could be brought into practice without upsetting the present structure. But imperialism thought otherwise. It wanted to coerce the people to do its will and did not seek any co-operation. Imperialism was blind to the moral prestige in the world.

Thus the struggle went on, mentally as well materially, until new ideas began to surge in the masses. By the time Vijaya Lakshmi had spent her four solitary months in the prison, the Monster of War in Europe had walked many miles and the international horizon had changed a great deal. India walked with the world and its masses were getting beyond the grip of the official noose. While the leaders made uncertain decisions, the masses were making up a certain mind. In the long run the Congress followed the people. And Vijaya Lakshmi Pandit followed the Congress. The leaders and the led were being shepherded by the hand of destiny to the goal of Complete Independence which though ever escapes our grasp like will-o'-the-wisp, has never been beyond the ken of our vision.

CHAPTER EIGHTH

India on the War-Path

In the blossom-land Japan,
Somewhere thus an old song ran,
Said a warrior to a smith,
" Hammer me a sword forthwith.
Make the blade
Light as wind on water laid.
Make it long
As the wheat at harvest song.
Supple, swift,
As a snake without rift,
Full of lightnings thousand-eyed !
Smooth as silken cloth and thin
As the web that spiders spin.
And merciless as pain and cold."
" On the hilt what shall be told ?"
"On the sword-hilt, my good man",
Said the warrior of Japan,
"Trace for me,
A running lake, a flock of sheep,
And one who sings her child to sleep."

SOLOMAN BLOOMGARDEN

(Translated from Hebrew by Marie Syrkin.)

When Britain was fighting out Fascism, India was grappling with Imperialism. Consequently, India kept clear of all fascist tendencies. Mahatma Gandhi and Jawaharlal, while in Europe, refused to interview Hitler and Mussolini. Nevertheless, the press reporters spread malacious accusations against them. Vijaya Lakshmi vigorously defended the honour of her brother in a statement issued from Allahabad on April 22, 1941.

I

LAKSHMI DEFENDS NEHRU

The following statement regarding Pandit Jawaharlal Nehru's visit to Munich in 1938 was issued by Mrs. Vijaya Lakshmi Pandit :

" Some newspapers have published what purports to be the translation of an article by Dr. Narayan Dutt Vidyalankar in the Hindi journal ' Ap Biti,' regarding my brother Jawaharlal Nehru's visit to Munich in August 1938. I have read this with amazement as part of it is entirely fanciful and I cannot imagine how Dr. Vidyalankar could have made himself responsible for certain statements which are patently false.

" I happened to meet my brother in Europe two weeks after his visit to Munich and he had told me what had happened there. In order to confirm my own recollection and to verify the facts, I asked him about them again in the course of a recent interview in prison, and drew his attention to Dr. Vidyalankar's statement. He expressed his great surprise at various untrue and imaginary references in this statement and asked me to correct them. Neither during his visit to Munich nor at any other time did he interview Dr. Goebbels and have any kind of communication with him. Nor did he receive at any time then, before or later, any letter or communication from Herr Hitler.

LAKSHMI IN LONDON
Meeting friends of the India League, along with Mrs. B. Batlivala, at the Finsbury Town Hall, London, on October 13, 1938.

LAKSHMI AGAINST LONDON
delivering a fighting speech at Lucknow against Viceroy's declaration of war on behalf of India in 1939.

THE STAR OF LIBERTY

Mrs. Vijaya Lakshmi Pandit caught by the camera-man as she was emerging from the U.S. transport planes at Karachi on her return from U. S. A.

"There are many other minor misstatements in Dr. Vidyalankar's account but it is hardly worth while to correct them. I might add that my brother knew Munich tolerably well as he had twice previously visited that city and stayed at the Hotel Vier Jahre Leiten. On this occasion also he had himself written to engage rooms in this Hotel."

II

WHAT ABOUT INDIA?

Everywhere, at every step, the British statesmen were heckled with embarrassing questions. Britain could not peacefully talk of freedom and democracy, while it was being denied to India. The common people in England had a great sympathy for the aspirations of India, but these were being hampered by the British imperialists. They put snares in the way of India's democracy. Miss Indira Nehru, the niece of Vijaya Lakshmi, clarified the British attitude on April 24, 1941, two days after the statement-in-defence issued by herself.

The story of Mr. C. R. Attlee, leader of the British Labour Party, who was booed off the platform at a Welsh miners' meeting when he waxed eloquent over democracy and freedom but could not answer a pointed reference to India, was related by Miss Indra Nehru in the course of a special interview to a representative of the Free Press Journal.

Mr. Attlee was interrupted, she said, and a voice rang out, "You talk of democracy and freedom; but what about India?" Mr. Attlee was silent. He was hissed off.

Mr. Attlee, it might be mentioned here, was not only a member of His Majesty's Cabinet, but also the Lord President of the Council, and belonged to a party which was pledged to grant freedom to India.

Similar incidents, she revealed had marred many a Labour meeting held in England of late. There was a cleavage of opinion between the leadership of the Labour Party and the rank and file. And more often than not the bone of contention was India.

Referring to the scandalous way in which the top men of the party had prevented Mr. V. K. Krishna Menon from standing on the Labour ticket for a seat of Parliament, she said, " They wanted to expel him too ; but then he changed them by resigning in time."

The common people in England who knew anything about India, she said, had great sympathy for this country's aspirations. Among them were workers and students. But politicians, whether of the diehard school or the Socialist brand, were quite indifferent to India's demand for freedom.

She smiled at the suggestion made in certain quarters that there was a change of heart in Britain's leaders towards India and remarked. " They say so. It seems they are prepared to grant Dominion Status. But then it remains to be seen to whom it will be granted—to the Viceroy or the people of this country."

Miss Indira Nehru, it might be remembered had been out of this country for nearly two years. When the war started she was in Switzerland recouping her health. Then for some time her whereabouts were not known and it caused not a little anxiety to her father, relatives and well-wishers. After the French collapse she travelled to Portugal through unoccupied France and from there she flew to England. A few months more and she left for India, arriving here only that week.

She did not seem to have improved much in health and the strain of the long journey had not been without its bad effects.

In common with her father she had a tendency to be outspoken in her comments. And had the times been better and freer she would have been glad to say many more things than have been published here.

"I might say many unprintable things" was how she threatened the representative of this paper when he met her. But in actual talk, she appeared to be singularly guarded.

Speaking about the newspapers of England she said that all the news about India that got past the censor's blue pencil and appeared in them related only to the war-effort in this country. To one who read those papers it would appear she remarked that there was nothing beyond a gigantic war-effort going on here. When any prominent person was arrested, he was honoured with a line or two in some insignificant corner. Thus an impression was sought to be created that the present satyagraha movement was a mere wash-out.

As for the politicians they seemed to have persuaded themselves that all was well in Hindustan. But then she had no doubt that American opinion was being definitely influenced in favour of India so much so that efforts were being made by the British Government of late to put the official version of the story before that country.

Asked as to where she came to know of her father's arrest, she replied, "in Switzerland. I got it first on the radio and then read a line about it in the papers."

The Swiss Government, in her opinion, is so conservative that very little sympathy is being felt there for India's struggle for freedom. In fact, she recalled how even when such a "meek man" like Gandhiji visited that country on his way to the Round Table Conference, Swiss newspapers had come out with the headline, "we do not want revolutionaries." She further said that no progressive movement was being allowed to grow there.

Questioned if she had had any real taste of an air-raid, she answered in a meek serious tone: "I think my presence here today is proof enough that bombs didn't fall right on my head though they fell pretty close to me. When I went to England the worst phase of air-attacks was already over. Even then, when there were raids during night time, I am afraid I never left my bed or flat. But when attacks came during day time, I went about my work as if nothing had happened."

She was all praise for the gallant way in which Britain was 'inking it' and said, "being used to such things, the people were never hysterical." She felt that there was shortage of food stuffs among the poorer sections.

To a question as to what opinion British people had about the Muslim League and its Pakistan demand, she stated, "I am afraid none at all. All they know is about the Congress and its struggle."

"What more interesting experiences have you to relate?" was one representative's next question: but before he could get an answer, good old Mr. Upadhyay, Panditji's secretary cut him off with the remark. "She will write all that in the form of an article later on." Rescued at last from an insatiable news-pest by her father's dutiful secretary she bade a hasty but courteous farewell.

III

EVENTS IN INDIA

The minister's room furnished with bluish green carpet!

Curtains to match! and " Khurja " bowls filled with roses perched around the 'angled' ebony table! Now the dark and dingy prison cells! What a drastic change! And yet that is the lot which nationalists in India have to face. That is what Vijaya Lakshmi suffered.

With the oncoming of the war all Congress ministers had tendered resignations. She acted according to the instructions from the Congress High Command. The political atmosphere in the country was tense. Gandhi started symbolic or individual satyagraha—a sort of " Socio-metaphysical " move from the Mahatma. The significance of this the youth of India have failed to understand.

Pandit Jawahar Lal issued historic 'ultimatum' to the British Government. He asked them to explain the principles and the objectives for which they were fighting. It would have enabled the Congress to decide whether to support the Allies in the war! Cripps Mission ended in smoke. These were the most vital events in the Indian politics.

The atmosphere in the country was explosive. Both the Government and the Congress were heading towards a terrible clash. Things came to a climax. And there came the Disturbances of the year 1942.

VIJAYA LAKSHMI PANDIT WITH OTHER SOLDIERS OF FREEDOM

The most important events of 1942 are the visit of Generalissimo and Madame Chiang Kai-Shek to India, the Cripps' mission and the Quit-India Movement. On the family front of Vijaya Lakshmi Pandit the most memorable event has been the marriage of Miss Indira Nehru, the only daughter of Jawaharlal.

The Nehrus of India have been personal friends of the Chiangs of China. Consequently, they took a great part in welcoming the leaders of China. Mrs. Vijaya Lakshmi Pandit organised a public reception for Madame Chiang under the auspices of All-India Women's Conference at the Lady Irwin College on February 12, 1942. Mrs. Vijaya Lakshmi Pandit read the welcome address and Madame Chiang replied to it in suitable words.

" Mrs. Pandit," said Madame Chiang, " sometime ago invited me to visit India, but owing to work I did not feel that I ought to leave China just then. The inward urge that I should come has been, however, latent for a long time, Therefore, when the Generalissimo decided to take this trip, this urge became crystallised into action. Now that I stand here in the midst of the women leaders of India, who like their Chinese sisters are making immense contributions to their beloved land in this hour of trials and tribulations, I am happy.........

" Mrs. Pandit has paid me a tribute for my share in the war of resistance to aggression. While appreciating this, may I have your permission to share this tribute with my fellow countrywomen ?........"

" War is at your very doors. As I came up from Calcutta to Delhi and saw your beautiful country and fertile lands I prayed that you should never have to suffer what we have suffered in China," said Madame Chiang Kai-Shek in a stirring address delivered 'ex tempore' to the meeting of women held on Thursday to give her public reception. She made the speech after her formal reply, to Mrs. Pandit's address of welcome.

"But," Madame Chiang Kai-Shek went on, " if you are to escape this fate you must be prepared to defend yourselves, for only by preparedness can you survive. First of all I want to tell you what you are up against, and I think you would want to know. I believe you are realists, for, in spite of thousands of years of our heritage enriched by the development of the most profound systems of philosophy yet evolved by any people in the world, the people of China and India are realists. You may have to fight against a foe full of treachery. During the last five years I have repeatedly pointed out what sort of people the Japanese are and what they have been doing in China, but because the western world was too engrossed in other affairs, they branded my admonitions as propaganda. Now that the world has had a taste of Japanese methods at Singapore and Manila they are realising that what I said was not a figment of war-torn imagination but bare facts. In 1932 at Shanghai when Chinese and Japanese had agreed in principle on certain conditions and were on the eve of signing an agreement, that very night the Japanese bombed and set fire to the sleeping population of Chapei and tens of thousands of people were killed and wounded."

Marshal and Madame Chiang Kai-Shek received press representatives in the garden of their residence in the Viceregal estates and spoke to them for a few minutes.

The Marshal, a little figure in dark flowing Chinese robes, greeted the gathering with simple dignity and friendliness and shook hands with each, looking straight at each with the quick, direct gaze of the man accustomed to size up people at a glance.

Madame Chiang went round with her husband, greeting them with a warm and cordial hand-shake.

" Madame Chiang and myself are very happy to meet you to-day," said the Marshal in Chinese, which was translated by Dr. Hollington Tong. " I have been in India for nearly a week, but what I have seen has tremendously impressed me. After my return to China, I may have something to say to you, but I have nothing to say now except to give you greetings. It gives me great pleasure to meet you to-day."

"You may ask a few questions to Madame Chiang," he added, to Madame's great merriment. "With your permission I will now retire. Good-bye."

Madame Chiang Kai-Shek cheerfully submitted to questions, and was asked to sum up her impressions said in English :

"I have been so short a time here and India is such a huge country that it is going to take me some time really to digest what I have seen. But one thing which has impressed me, one of the many things which has impressed me, is the fact that the women of India, like the women of China, will have to take a tremendous part in the reconstruction of the country.

"I have met quite a number of leaders among Indian women and I am full of hope that the women of India will be able to fulfil that destiny and I am greatly impressed by the selfless quality of the women whom I have met. And if they are the representatives of Indian women, I assure you, India has an even more glorious future than her past has been."

Giving her message to the Indian Press, she observed : "War has to be fought not only with bullets and with artillery and aeroplanes ; it has to be fought by the Press. You have tremendous influence over the people. The Press in China to-day reflects the will of the people, the heart of the people : not only does it reflect that, the Press is also the moulder of opinion. And you have, therefore, a tremendous responsibility. Voices die out, but the printed word seems to live on in the mind of the reader.

"I hope you will not take the easy way of writing the sensational, but the more fundamental and honest way o writing what you think the people should know in order to educate mass opinion. That is my message to you."

Speaking for my husband and myself we would have regretted it if we had not been able to see you because we feel that you are a very vital part, a very essential part, in the India of to-day and in the India of to-morrow."

Answering questions, whether there were religious differences in China, Madame Chiang said : "We have no clear-cut religious sections as in India. Religion has, more or less, become part of life. Politics is not coloured by religion. We are all Chinese. We are all one."

"It has been possible to put up this gigantic struggle," she said in reply to other questions, "because we feel it is better to die than to become slaves and to have our children and children's children become slaves, because we are determined to see that China is once for all freed from Japanese aggression."

"I am not paying you a compliment," she added, "but I feel a bond of sympathy and spiritual unity between your people and mine which my stay here has intensified."

Asked about the Taj, she said : "I think it is a beautiful building. I think it is the symbol of a spirit even more beautiful than the building itself; because it shows that none of us really die, even if our bodies die. I think the spirit lives on and when we think of the fact that so many centuries ago there was this devotion of an emperor to his empress, it only proves what the human heart and the human mind is capable of."

IV

A FAMILY INTERLUDE

In the weather-beaten days of 1942, there was a brief interlude in the family of the Nehrus at Anand Bhawan.

It was the marriage of Miss Indira, the daughter of Jawaharlal and the niece of Vijaya Lakshmi. Although a leader of the younger generation of the Nehrus, she have had the advantage of having been brought up by the elder Nehrus. If Krishna took her place after Vijaya Lakshmi, Indra took her plaçe after Krishna. Her marriage in a way closed the generation of Pandit Motilal's magnificent household. The coming Nehrus have been brought up in the cradle of nationalism. Miss Indira marks a stage of great importance between the death of aristocracy and the birth of democracy among the Nehrus. The following news-item appeared from Allahabad on February 26, 1946 :

" The engagement is announced of Miss Indira Nehru, the only daughter of Pandit Jawaharlal Nehru, with Mr. Feroz Gandhi.

" The marriage will take place in about a month's time at Allahabad.

" Mr. Feroze Gandhi, a young Parsi, is the brother of Mrs. T. K. Gandhi, personal assistant to the Chief Inspectress of Schools, United Provinces.

" Mr. Gandhi has travelled extensively in Europe and was in Spain during the Civil War. He was associated with the London Office of the National Herald and returned to India only a few months ago. He had first-hand experience of the present war.

" Mr. Gandhi has been a friend of the Nehru family for sometime.

" Miss Indira Nehru has been a student at the Cambridge University, Pandit Nehru's old university. She was convalescing in Switzerland. It may be recalled, after protracted illness when the present war broke out, it was with difficulty that she managed to return to India *via* Spain and London last year."

PT. JAWAHARLAL NEHRU'S STATEMENT

"The marriage is a personal and domestic matter affecting chiefly the two parties concerned and partly their families. Yet I recognise that, in view of my association with public affairs, I should take my many friends and colleagues and the public generally into my confidence," said Pandit Jawaharlal Nehru, in a statement to the press on the engagement of Miss Indira Nehru with Mr. Feroze Gandhi.

Pandit Nehru continued :

"I have long held the view that, though parents may and should advise in the matter, the choice and ultimate decision must lie with the two parties concerned. That decision, if arrived at, after mature deliberation, must be given effect to and it is not the business of parents or others to come in the way. "When I was assured that Indira and Feroze wanted to marry one another, I accepted willingly their decision and told them that it had my blessing.

"Mahatma Gandhi, whose opinion I value not only in public affairs but in private matters also, gave his blessing to the proposal.

"The members of my family as well as the members of my wife's family also gave their willing consent.

"Feroze Gandhi is a young Parsi, who has been a friend and colleague of ours for many years and I expect him to serve our country and our cause efficiently and well. But, on whomsoever my daughter's choice would have fallen, I would have accepted it or been false to the principles I have held.

"I hope and trust that this marriage will be a true comradeship in life and in the larger causes that we hold dear.

"Mahatma Gandhi expressed a wish that the marriage might take place in Sevagram so that he might find it convenient to be present at it and bless the union personally. We appreciated and were grateful for his suggestion, but the members of my family felt that the ceremony should take place in our home.

"The marriage will take place in about a month's time at Allahabad.

"I am not in favour of the pomp and circumstances that so often accompany marriages in our country. In present circumstances, when national and international crises envelop us, this would be particularly inappropriate."

The marriage of Miss Indira Nehru was performed with great pomp and show. Anand Bhawan was gaily lit up and was humming with activity. The palatial house of Motilal Nehru wore a festive appearance.

"It felt good," says Krishna, "to be back in old familiar surroundings and to see Jawahar, my sister, and others again."

Vijaya Lakshmi, Krishna, and Jawaharlal met together for a few happy days. And that was the chief pleasure for the children of Motilal. The loved house was no longer the same. So many dear ones were absent. But the present was a happy occasion for all of them.

"Though the passing of the years," says Krishna, "had wrought havoc in the home that once was full of happiness and peace, it was still good to be back, to feel the warmth of a brother's love, a sister's care and to feel a carefree girl of eighteen once again."

Vijaya Lakshmi has always bestowed a sister's care on Krishna since the departure of their governess. And little wonder, she remembers Vijaya Lakshmi lovingly in her autobiography.

The wedding day dawned. Everything was bright and beautiful. Many cousins and friends flocked to the bride's place. Indira was escorted by Jawaharlal to the pavilion where the marriage ceremony was performed. Everything went off beautifully.

V

AN INTERLUDE IN NON-VIOLENCE

It was August 1942. Gandhiji, to the astonishment of everybody, launched Quit-India Movement.

Vijaya Lakshmi took to her post of duty. She played her role in the battle for freedom. The Britishers call it "Rebellion." For that matter they may label it as India's Second Revolution.

Day and night she rushed about in the whirlwind. She faced stormy politics. Often she was dazed and tired. Now here and now there.

The whole country was agog with political upheavals. Indian nationalists, tired of endless waiting, decided to cast off the yoke of bureaucracy at any cost. They came to open rebellion. "Quit-India!" became the slogan. "Do or die" was the watchword. People were mad with fury against the repressive Government. They cut off telephone wires. They derailed the trains. They set the offices on fire. On the contrary the bureaucracy was bent upon crushing fiery patriotism. Lathi charges, firings and indiscriminate machine-gunning became the order of the day.

Lakshmi toured from place to place. She tried to check the excited masses. They were bent upon wreaking revenge upon the high-handed Government. Her appeals were of little avail. Mass feelings were pent up. They would not be pacified and bridled.

In the face of indiscriminate firings she rushed among the crowds. She helpled to pick up the wounded. She arranged for their removal to the hospitals.

At 2 a.m. on the 12th of August, 1942, she was awakened. The police authorities had come to arrest her. They were waiting for her with warrants.

"The police had arrived," she says. " It was 2 a.m. My mind was a confused jumble of events of the preceding twenty-four hours. The shots fired on the student's procession were still ringing in my ears and before my eyes I could only see the faces of those young men whom I had helped to pick up and remove to hospital. I was utterly weary in mind and body and more than a little dazed."

Her daughters were asleep at the hour. And she didn't like to disturb them. She went up to the porch. She switched on the light. She found that some police officers with quite an army of constables had come up to the verandah. This annoyed her.

" Why is it necessary for so many armed men to come to arrest one unarmed woman ? " She asked, ordering them to get off the verandah.

The girls were awakened. And she broke the news to them. " They were brave as always and immediately grasped the situation – no useless questions, no fuss."

All three of them helped her to pack things. Rita looked at her mother with big eyes heavy with sleep. Looking at the child, mother's courage began to ebb. She was so little and the world was so big—who would take care of her ?"

"I wish I could go to jail too" said Rita. "Mummie darling take care of yourself. We shall be fighting the British outside while you are in."

"Darling don't worry, everything will be fine," said Lekha embracing her mother.

Several police lorries were lined up on the roadside. She was shown into one of the lorries and driven off to Naini jail. After half an hour's waiting, the door of the female prison opened. She was conducted to the old familiar barrack. There she spread her bedding on the ground. A new term of jail life began.

After 9 months' imprisonment, she was set free on the 11th June, 1943 on grounds of ill health.

Jail confinement affected her health. The misery and vigour of jail made her look ten years older. She looked worn-out and rugged. Mrs. Krishna Hutheesingh saw her after the release.

"With sinking heart," she says, "I got out of the tonga and went in search of Swarup. As I entered her room she got up to greet me and embrace me. I put my arms around her trying not to let her see how moved I was at her changed appearance. A year ago I had seen her looking ten years younger than she really was. Nine months she had been in jail and was out for a few short weeks now. Once more jail had wrought havoc on a loved one and left its mark all too plainly on the face which had aged considerably in those few months."

But it was a very short interlude between the loving sisters. She had come out on a brief parole for a fortnight after nine months' imprisonment. And now she must return to her home in His Majesty's prison. Krishna describes the event touchingly.

"I stayed for a week,"* says Krishna, "and then returned to my home, my children and an existence without my dear ones. Swarup had to return to jail for an indefinite period leaving her three young daughters outside to fend for themselves as best they could, in a world where bitterness and frustration had taken the place of hope and happiness."

Only a mother's heart knows how painful it is to leave behind her children in the crowds of humanity. Krishna has written another magnificent passage on the destiny of Anand Bhawan. It refers to her arrival at Allahabad to see Vijaya Lakshmi :—

"A year passed. Once again I was on my way to Allahabad. This time to spend one short week with my sister Swarup, who after nine months' imprisonment was out on parole for a fortnight. Late at night I arrived at the familiar station, looking a little more dilapidated than it had done the last time. A friend and a young niece, Swarup's daughter, met me and we drove home, not in a car because there was no car any longer, but in a rather ancient tonga which seemed to crawl along the bad roads."

Hundred and thousands were lying behind the prisons. And Lakshmi was among them. The Second World War had engulfed the whole humanity. The Indian Nation was denied its freedom. Consequently the Indian nationalists were thrown into the cauldron. The masses of India had to fight against Fasicsm as well as imperialism. The British promises had many ifs and buts. Therefore, India had to fight against Britain while Britain was fighting against Germany.

At last Lakshmi was released on grounds of health.

Even then she looked for no rest. She took up the famine Relief work. She became the president of the " Save the Children " Fund Committee started by the All-India Women's Conference.

VI

THE WOMAN WARRIOR

Outside or inside Vijaya Lakshmi had no rest. Rest, as Jawaharlal said, is a betrayal of the masses who never rest. The political struggle must be carried on through sickness or death. Through sickness and sorrow the Indian patriots fight on, and if one man died another takes his place. Through all the calamities of life, including the death of her dear husband, Vijaya Lakshmi has never rested her forehead on her oar. She has regarded Freedom as the first line of defence and for that she has spared neither health nor wealth, neither her husband nor her dear children. She truly possesses the spirit of the great man Motilal Nehru. Shoulder to shoulder she has fought along with Jawaharlal. And being a woman has not bridled her activities.

In one of her stories she mentions an incident. She was persuading a very respectable lady to take interest in matters concerning the welfare of the country. Thereupon the respectable lady completely lost her temper. She retorted in anger :

" Why should I leave my home and go out to do political work ? Is it not my duty to serve my husband and give him sons ? Why should I bother about freedom for the country?"

Vijaya Lakshmi replied that in that way she would not only be able to serve the people. She will also have the opporturity of having more personal freedom. The lady was all the more perturbed and said :

"I have as much freedom as a decent woman askes for. It is only women like you, who have left your homes, who talk about freedom."

Vijaya Lakshmi Pandit tried in vain to remind her that she had not quitted her home. She had the welfare of her children and husband as much at heart as she. But the argument fell flat on her.

The remarks of the lady about Vijaya Lakshmi Pandit represent the ideas of a certain section of society in India. It constitutes mostly the uncompromising old fanatics. They would never come out of the traditional ways of thought. They think as their forefathers did. A woman's place, for them, is essentially in the home. There is no reason why she should perform the duties of a statesman. Even highly educated men sneer with disdain. If she became a minister, they say, she neglected her duties as a wife and mother. Her place was not in the minister's office but in the kitchen.

With such intellectual dwarfs argument and reason do not go far. None but the mentally impoverished would deny that as a political worker, she has contributed tremendous good to the society. If she had stuck to the traditional rut she would not have contributed anything good.

During the uncertain days of 1945, she did great service to India by presenting our case at the San Francisco Conference. She advanced India's case. The need for it was the greatest. Who else could do it? She did India great benefit. She decided to stick to her guns and the truth. She thundered with vigour and courage.

What Jawaharlal can do, Lakshmi can also do. The character of Motilal is exhibited in her as much as in her brother. Although Vijaya Lakshmi is a woman, she lives manfully. And the strength of her character has surprised even Mahatma Gandhi.

Vijaya Lakshmi is enraged to know that Britain which fights for the freedom of others has chosen to deny the same to India. Throughout the war she was torn between her sympathy for the British people and her hatred of the British politicians. Naturally she asked, along with her brother a clear declaration of Britain's war aims.

It was a mockery to ask the people of India to shed their blood without a clear promise of freedom. India wants to get rid of imperialism and also help other oppressed people to accomplish the same. It is this ideal to which Vijaya Lakshmi has devoted her life under the leadership of Mahatma Gandhi. And she has done the job without neglecting the humbler duties of life.

She never disregarded her duties as a wife and as a mother. Her prison experiences published under the name " The Prison Days " present her personality. She is perfectly human. Being separated from her husband and children she constantly indulged in sweet memories. Even she felt panicky about their welfare.

Her husband's health worried her ;

" I have had no news of Ranjit since he left for Bombay, three weeks ago and am beginning to worry about him. I wish I could communicate with him and tell him to be careful about his health."

Hope of an interview with her husband kept her happy :

" I have permission to interview Ranjit to-morrow. I am so excited."

And a brief interview did not please her ; " Lekha and I interviewed Ranjit......how unsatisfying a prison interview is !"

The husband and wife were detained in separate wards of the same jail. The idea of Ranjit being somewhere, on the other side, awakened in her irresistable longings to see him.

" He is somewhere on the other side of the wall and yet how far away. I have such a longing to see and speak to him."

" I had been eagerly looking forward to seeing Ranjit on the 14th...I was on the point of breaking down when in walked Ranjit happy and full of spirits." " Hallow old girl : What's wrong—bad news from home ?" were his words. He came and put his arm around me and I collapsed."

Every hour among the Prison walls, she was anxions about the welfare of little Lekha, Rita. Tara, and others. She did not even forget the little Cairn terrier. The news of its illness made her run about hither and thither to arrange for medical aid.

She longed for her husband, and children, sister and brother. She wished she were in the home with the family. And yet there was a greater and nobler cause for the emancipation of 400 million souls of India. It compelled her to leave off her home and its comforts, Her parental obligations were unperformed. But human mind has evolved much above the old and worn out conception. Only husband and children were not the objects for a woman to live and labour for. Husband and children form the circle—immediate around us ! Modern thinker refuses to be circumscribed by the limitation of the family. A woman has her duties as a wife and as a mother too. But there is a greater cause. It is the cause of the one-fifth of the humanity. The entire world is a big family.

Nehrus have always regarded the whole mankind as their home. And Vijaya Lakshmi has very well lived up to the traditions of the family. For the cause of Democracy she has fought in the thickest of the battle. And by Democracy the Nehrus means Democracy for everybody and not for India alone.

" We wish to get rid of imperialism," says Krishna, the sister of Vijaya Lakshmi, " not only where it concerns us, but wherever it exists throughout the world. Our freedom is but a symbol of that force, that desire to rid the rest of the world as well as ourselves of foreign domination and exploitation."

Quit-India Movement was an appeal to British conscience. But the British politicians turned a deaf ear. The issue was Liberty and Equality for all the nations. Without this ideal the World War was a mockery. And the leaders of India had no mind to delude themselves. And so the patriots of Mother India played their part. And Vijaya Lakshmi dignified her family and honoured the womankind. By her sacrifices the women of the globe have more plumes to their bonnets.

CHAPTER NINTH

Behind The British Bars

Even now
I seem to see my prison walls come close,
Built of darkness, and against that darkness
A girl no taller than my breast and very tired,
Leaning upon the bed and smiling, feeding
A little bird and lying slender as ash-trees,
Sleepily aware as I told of the green
Grapes and small bright-coloured river flowers.

—BILHANA.

(Translated from Sanskrit by E. P. Mathers).

Prison has become a second home for Mrs. Vijaya Lakshmi Pandit. Like a bird of passage she has flown between Anand Bhawan and Naini Jail in season and out of season. Her name is in the black registers of the British Government. And usually it does not take the police officials five minutes to clip her wings. It does not require any effort to spread a net for her. She flies head-wise into the British cage. That is what Gandhiji has taught his followers. And a British prison has ceased to be a house of terrors for the patriots. Not that there is any lack of tortures in the British cells. Certainly not. The patriots have simply ceased to mind them.

Those who have any doubt about the inconveniences of jail life should read Vijaya Lakshmi Pandit's *Prison Days*. The book describes the life of an 'A' Class Prisoner. Consequently it hardly gives the hardships of an ordinary type of a political worker. The hardships of a nationalist-in-the-street prisoner are real, not imaginary. Therefore, Vijaya Lakshmi thinks that her little diary is of no special importance.

"But," says Vijaya Lakshmi, "since the period from August 1942 onwards was enveloped in darkness and many people still have no idea what prison life means, this may help in giving a picture of the conditions prevailing in one of the better run jails of the United Provinces.

"The treatment given to me and to those who shared the barrack with me was, according to the prison standards, very lenient—the reader must not imagine that others were equally well treated. When the truth about the unhappy period is made known, many grim stories will come to light, but that time is still far off."

The above criterion must be borne in mind before plunging into the depths of Vijaya Lakshmi Pandit's experiences.

I

GOODBYE, GIRLS !

The police knocked Mrs. Lakshmi Pandit out of her bed at the most unearthly hour (2 a.m.) on August 12th—four days after the Quit-India Resolution and three days after the round-up of topmost Congress leaders, including Gandhiji and her brother Jawaharlal.

At two o'clock in the morning anybody's mind would be a jumble of events. So was Lakshmi's. The shots fired on the students were still whizzing in her ears.

The daughters of Mrs. Pandit were asleep. And she did not wish to disturb them. They had gone to bed quite done up. The sights of police terror had made them bewildered and unhappy.

Many armed men had come to arrest one unarmed woman. There was no one with the girls. And no arrangements could be made on the spur of the moment. Indira had arrived only a few hours earlier. So Lakshmi kissed her goodbye. Then she awoke the kiddies and broke the news. They took everything in a matter-of-fact spirit.

" Bye-bye Mummie darling," said Tara, " we shall keep the flag flying !"

Mrs. Pandit travelled along the smiliar road to Naini Prison. Before her mind floated like a film in a cinema the memories of other journeys. She had travelled to the British Bars over a dozen times since 1921. She was conducted to the old familiar barrack. Her head ached badly. The throbbing in her temple prevented sleep.

" There are few of the old familiar faoes left," writes she rather amusedly, " and the new ones look at me like something out of a museum."

II

A TALE OF NEGATIVES

The first day of Vijaya Lakshmi in Naini Prison was a tale of negatives.

NO information was sent to the jail authorities.

The jail staff did NOT expect her.

The jail matron was NOT present.

There was NO water.

There were NO sanitary arrangements.

The jail was UNABLE to supply rations.

Lakshmi had NO desire to accept the matron's tea.

Tea did NOT help her.

Raw rations came but NO coal.

Cooking was NOT possible.

Twig-fire would NOT light.

There was "In fact NOTHING at all," says the heroine. She could NOT read because of insects. On top of all, she could NOT sleep.

The same tale of negatives was repeated the next day.

"I awoke up in the morning feeling fresh and prepared to be civil to the world", says Vijaya Lakshmi," but when by 8. 30 a.m. there was NO coal and NO tea, I found myself losing temper. I think hunger had something to do with it also. The matron had NOT been, so I wrote and informed the Superintendent that since I had been admitted to the jail, NO food had been supplied to me and if it had NOT been for the matron's kindness in sending me some tea from her house I should have starved completely. I mentioned that if the jail was short of rations I might be given the cooked food served to the convicts."

Durgi was her helpmate. She was serving a sentence for the murder of her husband. She was dark but had pleasing features. She had nice limbs.

"I think," wrote Lakshmi, "she and I will be good friends."

When the rains fell cool and comfortable, the barrack was leaking badly, and there was NO spot where her bed could entirely escape.

"I have chosen a place," she says, "where my head is safe but where my feet will get a bath!"

But it rained in torrents. Her barrack looked like a lake. Her bed was an island.

"Coal" she writes, "is not supplied as on previous occasions and the smoke from the damp wood makes cooking very difficult. The rations are of the poorest quality and mixed with grit and dirt, tiny stones and even an odd spider or two thrown in for good weight. After cleaning the dal and rice one finds that the quantity has appreciably diminished. I am keeping the dirt I have taken out of my rations until inspection day and will show it to the doctor. The ghee supplied is dark brown in colour and has a funny smell. There is so little of it that it seems useless to bother about the quality."

Lack of news was irritating. A jail is a sort of whispering gallery. And the whispers have a habit of echoing and re-echoing.

Monday was the parade day. And it was the busiest day of the week. There was the usual hustle and bustle since dawn. There was shouting, abuse, and much running about. And finally, the visit of the Superintendent! It was very brief, thank goodness! Lakshmi Pandit was not in a mood for his small talk.

" Are you satisfied ?" asked the Superintendent.

" Would I be in jail if I were ? " asked the heroine.

"The Superintendent's remark," says Lakshmi, "gives me food for thought—satisfaction, comfort, happiness, freedom—how meaningless these words have become. I am inclined to agree with Bernard Shaw when he says : 'Only on paper has humanity yet achieved glory, beauty, truth, knowledge, virtue and abiding love.'"

Children sent her books on her birthday, but she could not enjoy them, because new regulations were imposed. She was put in the 'B' class prisoners.

" We shall not be permitted," she writes, " newspapers, letters or interviews or any article from home. Jail clothes will be provided—lock up will take place. Our allowance will be reduced from -/12/- to -/9/- per day."

None of these things moved Vijaya Lakshmi except the restriction on correspondence.

The saddest news that came to her was the death of Mahadev Desai, the private secretary of Gandhi.

III

A NATIONAL TRAGEDY

"The sad news" says Vijaya Lakshmi, "that Mahadev Desai had died of heart failure in jail on the 15th has come as a great shock and has deeply hurt me. My mind is full of pictures of him. He was a fine person—one of God's good men. We are the poorer for his loss. I wonder where poor, Durga and the boy are. Now that Bapu is in prison they have no home. I wish I could send a word of comfort to Durga. Ever since I heard of Mahadevbhai'sdeath I have been terribly upset. Last night I lay awake and so many incidents connected with him passed through my mind. It seems only the other day that he came to me in Anand Bhawan and asked me to read an article in the Moden Review written by a dear friend of his—a young man whom he described as most brilliant and very lovable. The year was 1920, the article was entitled *At the Feet of the Guru*, and the name of the author was Ranjit Pandit. For 22 years now I have been the wife of this most brilliant and most lovable man. Ranjit and Mahadev were at college together and graduated in the same year. Although they seldom corresponded, there was a deep bond of sympathy and affection between them. The news of Mahadev's passing will hurt Ranjit."

The place assumed gigantic proportions at night. The tiny flickering light of the jail lantern cast long and weird shadows. These have a ghostly appearance. Vijaya Lakshmi sat and looked at them. And she wove stories to amuse herself. The yard was the most dreary place imaginable.

" The number of frogs in the yard," says Lakshmi, " is unbelievable. They are all over the place — great big ugly creatures and incredibly foolish-looking. They remind me of war profiteers—those smug people who are so content with the little circle in which they move that they completely forget there is a world outside it."

The twinkling stars alone gave Lakshmi a feeling of security. They were always the same, sweet and serene. The follies of men did not worry them. Sometimes a moonbeam also stole in. It lay across the floor lake a silver stream.

" Occasionally I hear planes fly overhead," says Lakshmi, " the sound makes me feel restless. I want to break through my bars and fly. It is absurd to keep human beings locked up in this fashion—It solves no problems and creates new ones. The world moves in a circle and we always come back to the starting point. Progress is only a word ; what does it mean, I wonder."

IV

WHERE MEN ARE BURIED ALIVE

"A prison," said Geffray Mynahul, "is a grave to bury men alive, a place wherein a man for half a year's imprisonment may learn more law than he can at Westminister for a hundred pounds. It is a microcosm, a little world of woe, it is a map of misery, it is a place that will teach a young man more villiany if he be apt to take it in one half year, than he can learn at twenty bowling rallies, brothel houses or ordinaries; and an old man more policy than if he had been a pupil to Machiavelli. It is a place that hath more disease prominent in it than the pest-house in plague time and it stinks more than the Lord Mayor's dog-house in August."

Lakshmi quotes a rhyme to show the wretched state of the prison life :—

> "As he went through cold Bath Fields he saw a solitary cell.
>
> And the Devil was pleased, for it gave him a hint.
>
> For improving the prisons in Hell."

"I do not of course know," says Vijaya Lakshmi, "what the prisons in Hell are like but if I finally get as far as the Nether Regions, I shall be able to give the devil quite a few hints on their improvement after my growing experience of prisons in British India."

The prison days are incredibly long. The prison nights contain more hours than any others. Time lengthens out. Each day is a month. Each month is a year. One easily lives through a century. The Superintendent asked Mrs. Pandit as to how old she was.

"I do not know," she said. "I feel as if I had lived through centuries."

Mrs. Pandit was reminded of an excellent quotation "No hour glass, no diary can estimate for you the fullness of time; it is the soul that fills it: if the soul lie asleep, it is not filled at all; if it be awake, in the vigils of suspense, of sorrow, of aspiration there may be more in an hour than you can find in a dozen empty lives. It is not larger time that we want, so much as the more capacious soul to flow through every pore of the little that we have."

It was the more capacious soul, she thought, that made Lakshmi feel as if she had lived through centuries.

"Do you know," said the matron to Lakshmi, "when I unlock your barrack each morning I try not to disturb you because I know you do not sleep well at night. But I was thinking I should by right call out to you because, if you were to die at night, how should I know."

"She is," says Lakshmi, "I suppose, what one would call a Job's comforter. Happy thought that I should die in the night, yet I expect there are worse deaths!"

V

DAUGHTER FOLLOWS THE MOTHER

On August 30, 1942, Lekha, laden with flower garlands strode up to the mother. She announced in triumphant tones that she had been arrested. It came an almost unbelievable blow to the mother.

"Lekha arrested!" said Lakshmi. "Why surely Lekha was only a baby still not nearly old enongh to understand politics, let alone live it."

The whole history of Lekha flashed across the mind of Mrs. Pandit. She saw her as a chubby baby lying on the Juhu sand. Then terrible period of illness and a miraculous escape. Then Lekha at the railway station in 1912 when Mr. and Mrs. Pandit were arrested. She was silent and wide-eyed, blinking away tears and clutching a big tricolour flag.

"Don't carry that big flag darling," said Vijaya Lakshmi.

"It's to frighten the police away with," replied the little girl.

Then the mother saw the various pictures of her life until the day of her arrest.

When the clock was advanced by an hour, the prisoners were the real sufferers. This affected them adversely, because the lock-up took place one hour earlier. They lost one hour of freedom. And it was the best hour in the coolness of evening.

Once at midnight Lekha gave a shout. And she bounded out of her bed. A large bat from the roof had fallen on her chest. They got off the bed. But the bat kept circling for hours.

"Anyhow," says Lakshmi, "we were much too frightened to sleep well after that!" Who says prison life is lacking in thrills?

It was not long after that the niece of Vijaya Lakshmi was also brought to the same barrack. She was Miss Indira, the daughter of Jawaharlal. The husband of the girl also followed the Nehrus to the prison.

"The police arrived," says Lakshmi, "and made an attempt to arrest Indu and some others who were there. There was a scuffle between the crowd and the police. Indu was pulled about and bruised and had her clothes torn. Finally they were brought here. Feroze had also been arrested."

VI

HUSBAND FOLLOWS THE WIFE

The husband of Vijaya Lakshmi Pandit was arrested on September 19, 1942.

"Ranjit," says Lakshmi, "was arrested at 6 o'clock this morning at Anand Bhawan. He returned from Bombay the night before last. Poor Tara and Rita! I was hoping they would have at least a week with their father. But these days man proposes and the British Government disposes."

Shortly after, Lakshmi, Lekha and Indira were placed in 'A' Class. Ranjit and Dr. Katju were also so classified. Lakshmi was not prepared to accept this class and wrote to the Superintendent for explanation.

Ranjit sent his wife some seeds and cuttings. The garden he started in his barrack last year was still flourishing. He brought her a bunch of nasturtiums at their interview. The soil in the female prison was very stony. So the matron offered to get them a few flower-pots and boxes for sowing seeds.

"Lekha and I," says Lakshmi, "interviewed Ranjit. Found him looking bright in spite of the continuation of his foot trouble. It was good to see him again but how unsatisfying a prison interview is."

The Superintendent gave no reply regarding regular meetings between husband and wife in jail. An interview with Ranjit did Lakshmi great good. But the authorities never hurried about it.

"I hate meeting Ranjit in a crowd," says Lakshmi. "I forget all the things I had planned to say and the lack of privacy upsets me."

Flowers make a great difference to our temper and surroundings. The female prison had a few flower-pots sent by Ranjit, but Ranjit garden was flourishing due to his efforts.

Rita, the little daughter of Lakshmi, had come to see mother, but she was refused permission. This upset Lakshmi very much. It was the interview day with Ranjit. Ranjit walked in happy and full of spirits.

"Hello old girl!" he said. "What's wrong—bad news from home?"

Lakshmi collapsed. He pulled her up. Then she told her the distressing story.

"Do you mean to tell me," asked Ranjit, "you actually asked for permission to see Rita? Haven't I told you again and again that we cannot seek favours from these petty gaulieters who are placed in authority over us? You must not let your feelings get the better of you. You are much too big a person, my dear girl, to ask favours from anybody. There is no room in this struggle for softness or favours. Pull yourself up."

Ranjit finished translating the '*Ritu Samhara*', and read some passages to his wife. They were beautifully rendered.

The jail officials often forgot to arrange for interviews between Lakshmi and Ranjit at the appointed time. There was no sign of the matron at the fixed hour. She wondered why the jail officials, forgot the human psychology. Just a little thought would make life more pleasant.

"The old year ends to-day," wrote Lakshmi on December 31, 1942. "This time last year I was in Cocanada with Lekha and Tara, and Rita was spending her holidays in Bombay with Ranjit."

But now both of them were in prison with only a wall between them. Even Lekha had followed them to the British prison while Tara and Rita were leading a lonely life at home.

The couple observed a twenty-four hours fast in sympathy with Gandhiji's fast unto death in February 1943.

V

THE GIRLS GO ABROAD

In April 1943, Lekha was released during the parole of Vijaya Lakshmi. The mother discussed with her daughter the question of her joining Wellesley College. She was reluctant to leave India. And she argued against it. But Mr. and Mrs. Pandit wanted the girls to have the advantage of free education in a free country.

"I pressed my point," says Lakshmi, "and told her she would be in a far better position to serve India in a few years with the benefits that an American College and contacts with worthwhile people who are doing things, than in her present condition.

It is hard to curb the impatience of eighteen. But finally Lekha consented. It was decided that Tara should also go. Ranjit gave his whole-hearted support. Lakshmi cabled to her friends in the United States. The reply from the President of Wellesley College came in 48 hours :

" Wellesley College proud and pleased to welcome your daughters."

It was a big relief to the mother. She had to undertake a great deal of correspondence regarding dollar exchange, passports, etc. At last she saw the girls off to Bombay and drove back straight from station to her prison.

The parting was a difficult affair. Mother and the daughters were very near to tears. They went on talking of other things until the train steamed off.

" We shall keep the flag flying darling" said the girls, as they waved to mummy, " wherever we are. "

" I know," said Lakshmi to herself, " we have done right in sending them to the United States. They will have wider opportunities of development and will be well cared for."

Sending girls to America involved endless correspondence. What must the District Magistrate have thought about it? It must certainly have added to his work, and possibily detracted from his good temper !

On April 28, 1943 Lakshmi received a telegram from Bombay that there had been some mismanagement about passports. The matter was delayed. Meanwhile a ship was due to sail in a few days. Satisfactory replies had been received from U. S. A. Lakshmi could not understand exactly what she felt about it. She could not understand her own feelings. She wanted the girls to go. It seemed in their best interest so far as she had been able to figure it out. And yet as the time approached for departure, her heart was heavy with anxiety. Like every mother from the beginning of time she was torn between two desires. Immediate nearness fought with future good. Life is so difficult. There is the necessity to decide and compromise between things. She was thankful that her husband fully agreed with her.

The sisters sailed from India on May 15, 1943. The mother had been planning for their departure. And now she was unhappy. Her days were heavy with anxiety. Early in June Lekha and Tara arrived in Melbourne on their way to America. They had taken the longer route to keep clear of German U-boats. The heart of Lakshmi was heavy. Her mind was following her daughters on their journey. It was not long before she followed them herself.

CHAPTER TENTH

India's Ambassador in America

In my boat that goes
Over manifold salt-ways
Towards the open sea
Faintly I hear
The cry of the first wild-goose.

—SAIGYO HOSHI (JAPANESE POET).

While the beloved daughters of Mrs. Vijaya Lakshmi Pandit were in America, she was not feeling at home in India. So she took a boat that went over manifold salt-ways towards the open sea of America. It was the wintry month of November 1944. The first cry that she heard in New York came from Bajpai, Britain's " first wild goose " of anti-Indian propaganda in the U. S. A.

In India Mrs. Pandit had long fought against the British lions, but in America she had to chase the British geese. And she found that the latter is even more dangerous than the former. It is much more difficult to come to grips with a goose than with a lion. But the heroine of India outwitted the one as she had outwitted the other.

I

JOHN BULL FOOLS UNCLE SHAM

Mr. Chaman Lal, the well-known Indian journalist, who recently returned from America and was detained in Karachi for 15 days, made interesting revelations in this article about the systematic campaign in the U. S. A. against India.

The Government of India, according to him, spends about 2½ million rupees and the British Government about 10 to 12 million dollars every year for anti-Indian propaganda in America. About 10,000 persons are engaged exclusively in this mission of advocating the cause of British Imperialism in America.

America is the happy hunting ground for anti-Indian propaganda. There are nearly 10,000 British propagandists engaged in the work of slandering India.

Why is Great Britain spending millions of her money, as well as our money, in the anti-Indian propaganda? Because India looks to the liberty-loving people of America for sympathy and support in her struggle and Britain is determined to deprive us of the sympathetic moral support of the great American people.

No one knows exactly how much of this campaign is run at India's expense, because most of the funds spent from India are 'Secret Funds,' not votable by the Indian Legislative Assembly. It is, however, estimated that the Government of India spends approximately two and half million rupees a year and the British Government spends about ten to twelve million dollars a year for propaganda.

With the arrival of Sir Girja Shankar Bajpai as India's first Agent-General, and Mr. J. Hennesy as Information Officer, the office of the Agent-General in the U. S. became the centre of disseminating guidance on the lines of anti-India propaganda to the various British public agents.

Sources of inspiration in India until recently were Sir Frederick Puckle (now adviser to Lord Halifax) and Mr.

Joyce of the India Office. Mr. Hennesy started issuing releases to a large mailing list which was prepared with the co-operation of British Information Services. These releases were of three types :—

1. Vital guidance notes sent only to British officials and a number of well-tried and trusted pro-British Americans ; 2. Background materials which were confidential but which could be used publicly without revealing its source were sent to a somewhat wider clientele ; 3. Press releases sent to a public mailing list.

These three mailing lists all reached several thousands. The British Information Services have, of course, their separate mailing lists which run into hundreds of thousands of names. Hundreds of books, booklets and pamphlets have also been printed and circulated free by this "mis-information officer" of the Government of India.

Much of the propaganda is arranged and carried on through personal contacts, correspondence, informal talks to selected influential groups, and by radio talks, public meetings, etc. An endless stream of high-powered propagandists continues to flow from England every week by air and sea. They are sent around the country on schedules arranged in advance by the Secret Department of the British Information sources and the numerous British Consulates scattered throughout America. These propagandists, who include some members of the British Cabinet, make public speeches, give information talks, and try in every possible way to convince important groups of newspaper men, educationists, etc. etc., that England honestly intends to grant freedom to the people of India. Cocktail parties and tea parties at the British Embassy and British Consulates are specially arranged in honour of these distinguished propagandists and newspapermen, college professors, industrialists and other men of influence and high standing, are invited to meet them.

Sir Fredrick Puckle has met some important newspapermen of influence at cocktail parties and other functions in the large cities, and even in smaller towns with a population of 10,000, or so and of course endeavoured to prejudice their minds against India's cause for freedom, and I am sorry to say that some editors, who were erstwhile friends of India seem to have been 'won over' to the other side by these British propagandists, as the editorials of a well-known paper like "The Nation" show.

Besides the above-mentioned influx of British officers, about 30 Indians have been brought to the United States as propagandists.

It is officially estimated that there are about 10,000 British propagandists in the United States who are devoting their time exclusively to India.

There are also Britishers who have become naturalized citizens of America during the past 5 to 15 years, with the sole purpose and intention to infilterate into the American institutional groups—they continue to stress the necessity for the British Empire to continue its rule in India. These are often referred to as "Beaverbrook's Bright Boys", as it was originally Lord Beaverbrook's bright idea to send these men to America to capture key positions in the various walks of life. Practically every department of the U. S. Government has one or more of these ex-Britishers "Plantex" in key positions, and among those in this group actively carrying on anti-Indian propaganda are a thousand or more.

Then there are pro-British Americans, people with British associations and sympathies due to social, financial or family relationships, business interests and educational background (*e.g.*, Rhodes' Scholarships) etc. Many of these are American missionaries who have been in India and have been won over by the British through special favours such as Kesar-i-Hind medals, pats on the back by Governors and other high officials.

Mr. Chamanlal mentions a few of the above type :—

(1) Mr. and Mrs. Peter Muir were imported into India as guests of the Viceroy, Governors and Ruling Princes in 1942. They enjoyed our hospitality for 15 months, then brought out a most poisonous book entitled " This Is India ". The manuscript of his book was revised, checked up and rewritten in the United States by the British Information Services. The British Information Services and its Indian Appendage, purchased 30,000 copies of this book for free distribution.

(2) In this connection Chamanlal mentions Post Wheller, cousin of Miss Mayo. He has brought out a book entitled " India Against the Storm." He was a diplomat in the American Consulate stationed in India and was bought over by the British.

Recently such attempts at dispatching Americans to India have been made by the British Ministry of Information so that such American " Experts " can spend sometime in India and return as authorities on India and defame India before the American citizens :—

Mr. Archer, a Professor of the Yale University, was in India for 19 years and was recently requested to go back to India. Lord Halifax took personal interest in this matter. Mr. Archer, however, was discouraged by the American

Government and his trip did not materialize because the American Government felt that his trip to India would harm the reputation of the American people in India. This was a "Slap in the face of Lord Halifax."

The American Government seems to be much wiser than the American newspapermen, some of whom easily fall into the traps of the British Ministry of Information.

Among the leading American journalists who are openly championing the cause of the British Imperialism in the American press are:—Walter Lippman; Dorothy Thompson; Major Fielding Elliot; Phillip Simms; Waverly Root and Barnet Nover.

Their propaganda against India is rather subtle but I am glad to note that the vast majority of the American newspapers are openly for India's freedom and those above mentioned have miserably failed to prejudice the American opinion against India.

"Britain can't fool us" is the common remark on every American lip when you discuss the question of India with the majority of Americans, and the average American strongly resents and hates the propaganda that the British carry on to malign the cause of India in her fight for freedom.

In November 1944 Lakshmi sailed for the United States of America to see her daughters. Also she wanted to acquaint the American people with the true state of affairs in India. Hitherto all they came to know was through the vilifying propaganda in the U. S. A. by the agents of the British Government.

Americans had been made to believe that India was a land of Snake-charmers, and Astrologers, and Charlatans. Therein the 'natives' lived on trees. A gang of loyal puppets of the British Imperialism had propagated that India was a house divided against itself. The British were honestly trying to bring the irreconcilable elements together. If the British weren't there to police those communal forces, the country would be plunged in anarchy. And chaos would ultimately endanger the world peace. It was put forth that Mahatma Gandhi and the Congress were agents of Japan. The Congress was a Fascist body dominated by the Hindu capitalists. They wanted the British to quit India, so that they might establish a Hindu imperialism to exploit the masses.

The political differences in India had led into a stalemate. The Congress leaders were rotting in jails. Prices were soaring. Profiteering was in full swing. Starvation stared millions of Indians in the face. But John Bull fought the war.

The British Government has been verylavish in putting its side of the Indian case before the British and American public. What worried Vijaya Lakshmi Pandit was that the British diplomats kept everybody in the dark. Immediately after the Quit-India Resolution, Manuel Quezon brought up the Indian question before President Roosevelt. But due to vigorous British propaganda, American interest in India slackened. Louis Fischer lists the following arguments with which the British representatives in U. S. A. embellish the Indian situation —

(1) Two million Indians volunteered (stress on "volunteered") to serve in the British Army. They fought valiantly for the King-Emperor on many fronts in the Second World War. Surely this would not suggest that British rule in India has no popular support; quite the contrary.

(2) Indians are hopelessly divided. Hindus and Moslems constantly quarrel and bicker. Tension between them has grown

year by year. Moslems of India follow Mohammed Ali Jinnah and Jinnah wants Pakistan. If the British tried to give India independence without creating a separate Moslem State a bloody civil war would break out from one end of the subcontinent to the other. Moslems are the warriors of India. How in the circumstances can the British simply withdraw from India ?

(3) Hindus are cruel to untouchables and exploit Moslems.

(4) Great Britain has conferred many benefits on India. It has built railways, irrigated vast areas, introduced education, improved health conditions and taught Indians the democratic way of life. But Indians are an ungrateful people. They blame British but do nothing themselves to improve their condition. Chief problems of India arise from Indian superstitions and religious beliefs : the worship of the cow, for instance, early marriages, enforced widowhood, etc.

(6) The Bengal famine was due to war dislocations.

(7) Gandhi contradicts himself continually and there is no practical way of dealing with him. Nehru is radical and wants to introduce fundamental changes in agriculture and industry. He is also a visionary. Gandhi and Nehru have had sharp disagreements.

(8) The Congress Party is the chief source of the anti-British agitation in India. It is financed by big Indian millionaire industrialists.

(9) India has no leaders who could run a free India. The only real statesman is Mr. C. Rajagopalachari and he does not see eye to eye with Gandhi and Nehru.

(10) Although Asia is in turmoil India is an island of order and law.

(11) The British will get out of India as soon as Indians can evolve a satisfactory constitution.

(12) England has treaty obligations to the Princes and moral obligations to the minorities and must safeguard their interests before quitting India.

(13) The British want nothing from India. They merely wish to create a situation which will enable them to get out. If the British left India without setting up an adequate administration, the country might fall a prey to some other foreign nation, which would treat India much worse than the British have.

II

FRISCO OR FIASCO ?

The United Nations had fought Nazism for the principles of Democracy, Justice and Freedom. They liberated Europe from the shackles of Nazism and Fascism. They met at San Francisco, U.S.A., to draw out a charter for permanent peace in the world. His Excellency the Viceroy, nominated three Knights—Sir Feroze, Sir Mudaliar and Sir. Krishnamachari. All three of them are known as first class "yesmen" of the British Government, these were India's representatives in the San Francisco Conference. Nominated in a most undemocratic way, they were to be sent to the Assembly which met for the purpose of establishing a democratic charter for the peoples of the world.

And anxious were these prize-boys to exhibit their loyalty. It was evident from their faces. Even before leaving for U.S.A., Sir Feroze declared in a public meeting in London that India was already a "free" country, and had attained Dominion Status. Even His Majesty's Government was shocked. He maintained that Indian members of the Viceroy's

Executive Council pursued any policy they thought beneficial to the country. The Viceroy didn't interfere in the day-to-day operations of the Executive Council. These revelations evoked ridicule. Laughter rang from the educated classes in India. Sir M. Krishnamachari and Sir Feroze gave an interview to Mr. J. J. Singh in U.S.A. during the days of the San Francisco Conference. They tried to " enlighten " the Indian opinion. Their objective was to secure a permanent seat for India on the Security Council ! All that they had in view was the securing of another seat for Britain. Raising the issue of India's freedom was not in their pocket-books.

Sir Ramaswami said, " We are responsible to the Government of India, not His Majesty's Government." Did it matter whether he represented His Majesty's Government or the Government of India ? There is no more difference between tweedledum and tweedledee than between Britain and " India." He didn't represent his people.

Such puppets represented India at San Francisco. The people were naturally disappointed. They didn't expect much from the Conference. India's interest was not there. The only hope was the presence of Vijaya Lakshmi Pandit in America. She had decided to represent India's case to the Allied Nations Security Council in the form of a memorandum. All eyes were therefore turned towards her. And people looked up to her with wonder-waiting eyes.

Towards the end of April, 1945, she arrived at San Francisco. A leading English nationalist daily of Northern India observed in its editorial, " Now that Mrs. Vijaya Lakshmi Pandit is at San Francisco, her presence there must be giving the Indian delegation sleepless nights."

When she arrived at San Francisco, a group of her countrymen, Doctor Anup Singh and Mr. J N. Sharma and many others including women, some of whom had travelled as long as 900 miles, welcomed her and loaded her with garlands.

The first fire she shot at San Francisco was the declaration : " I desire to make it clear that the so-called Indian representatives attending the San Francisco Conference have not the slightest representative capacity. They have no sanction, no mandate from any of the responsible groups in India and are merely nominees of the British Government. Anything they say here or any vote they cast can have no binding effect or force on the people of India."

With reference to the Indian delegates Mr. Iftone, a correspondent, wrote, " They have been chosen by the Government without consultation of Indian parties or political leaders most of whom are still in jail including the far-seeing Nehru who would have shone even in a gathering of giants."

Sir Feroze and other Indian representatives to the San Francisco Conference, were aware of their own non-representative character. Their own conscience pricked them. Instead of facing Mrs. Pandit's challenge, they were feeling nervous. So they came down to tactics which were rather unbecoming. The titles which they carried about themselves became uncomfortable.

When Mrs. Pandit was giving a press conference, a fellow named Khurshid Ahmed Khan, a Stenographer attached to the Indian delegation—probably therefore Noon's stooge—tried to heckle her with meaningless questions. Mr. Pasbom, Associated Press of America representative, wired :—

" The heckler at Mrs. Pandit's press conference yesterday turns out to be Kurshid Ahmed Khan, a stenographer attached to the Indian delegation. I called upon him this morning. He would not talk. He said, 'I have told you I cannot answer any question. We are not supposed to give any interviews to the press.' Then I suggested, should not I understand that civil servants of the Imperial Secretariat are also not supposed to make demonstrations at press conferences? He just looked away and would not answer. I met some other Indian members of the staff including personal assistants to the delegates. They were all very courteous and pleasant. But poor Khurshid looked most unhappy, sour and belligerent.

"No one in India would believe that a civil servant, specially an ordinary stenographer, would have courage to get up and ask such questions before the world press unless he was instructed to do so. The question is which of the three delegates bungled and planted this man. Personally I think Sir Ramaswami Mudaliar is too shrewd to make such a mistake. Sir M. Krishnamachari too is placid for such machinations. That leaves only Sir Feroz Khan Noon. Naturally it could not be proved that he was responsible for this indiscretion.

"It does tie up with the threat Sir Feroze gave me which I reported earlier in a despatch that unless we 'propagandists' kept quiet they may be forced to retaliate.

"I must say that K. A. Khan was very badly coached. If his mentor had been smart he would have instructed him to put one question at a time avoiding obvious tactics of a heckler and should have been patient enough to wait till others had asked some questions instead of being the first. K. A. Khan's inability to control himself exposed him to newspapermen who spotted him as a heckler and were incensed when they found he was not a newspaperman. If K. A. Khan's boss had expected that the association of Indian delegation with this episode would remain a secret, then his boss does not know American newspapermen. They traced Khan and everyone knew within an hour that he was with the Indian delegation.

"It must have been most uncomfortable for his boss to learn to-day that the efforts of his 'stooge' instead of disrupting Mrs. Pandit's press conference have boomeranged and Mrs. Pandit has received much wider publicity both at the radio and press than she might have otherwise. Yesterday evening papers and this morning's papers have given her a prominent space with pictures. One paper had a big picture of Mrs. Pandit being garlanded by Amritlal Seth and a small picture of Khan with his name and 'ejected from conference.'

Mrs. Pandit interviewed that morning said : "I do think Khan's interruptions were a deliberate attempt to put a wrong emphasis on conditions in India which I was trying to depict."

It was proved that the fellow had been sent there by Sir Feroze to harrass Mrs. Pandit. It was a retaliatory measure against her challenge. Sir Feroze had no national character in the Conference. The efforts of the "stooge" were to disrepute Mrs. Pandit. But it boomeranged, and Mrs. Pandit received wider publicity than she would have otherwise expected. One of the papers published the heckler's photograph with specification of a disgraceful dismissal.

In May, 1945 Mrs. Pandit on behalf of the India League of America, and the National Committee for India's freedom submitted to the San Francisco Conference a memorandum. It called for an immediate declaration of India's independence.

III

MOST MEMORABLE MEMORANDUM

Mrs. Pandit, on behalf of the India League of America and the National Committee for India's Freedom, has submitted to the San Francisco Conference a memorandum calling for an immediate declaration of India's independence, says Reuter's Special Correspondent.

The memorandum describes the Indian problem as " the acid test of the principles on which the hopes of the conference are postulated. " It states that India's dependent status is " not only grave moral and political wrong to India but a travesty of the claim that the United Nations' conference consists of representatives of sovereign nations. The imperialist system should now be renounced in principle and abandoned in practice by an unequivocal acknowledgment and declaration of a free India. "

Mrs. Pandit declared that she spoke also for Burma, Malaya, Indo-China and Dutch Indies for whom she claims "liberation from all alien imperialism."

In the memorandum, which is submitted to the Secretary General of the United Nations' Conference, an international organisation, Mrs. Pandit described herself in a formal preamble as " Madame Vijaya Lakshmi Pandit, spokesman for India. "

The text of the memorandum added.

" As a member of the Indian National Congress party in India and one who has been selected to be the spokesman for India on the occasion of the United Nations' Conference for international organisation in San Francisco by the Indian League of America (which is an organisation predominantly of American citizens devoted to the cause of Indian freedom) and by the National Committee for India's freedom (which represents a vast majority of Indian nationals resident in United States) I desire respectfully to submit the following observation and representations with a request that you place them before the members of the delegation of the United Nations now assembled in the Conference. "

As M. Molotov mentioned at his press Conference on April 30 " We have at this Conference an Indian delegation. But India is not an independent state. We all know a time will come when the voice of independent India will be heard too. Nevertheless we share the view held by the British Government that the representatives of India should be granted a seat at the Conference, imperfect though her status is".

The memorandum continued " The fact that the head of the delegation of one of the four sponsoring nations at this conference has pointed out firstly that India is not an independent state, secondly there is a delegation present at this conference from India which was invited at the request of the British Government and thirdly he understands that sometime in the future, the voice of India will be heard provided an opportune moment for the discharge of necessary duty, (namely, to draw the attention of the United Nations' Conference to the problem of India, which is at once the acid test of the principles on which the hopes of the Conference are postulated and a cancerous menace to the prospects of lasting concord and harmony among nations is removed after the labours of this Conference, as we all hope, are fruitfully concluded.

A FEW ESSENTIAL FACTS

"Let me recapitulate a few essential and inescapable facts. India to-day comprises 400 million people naturally and necessarily consisting of various racial and cultural groups and with geographical area of almost the size of the continent of Europe. Nevertheless India is a geographical unit, cultural unit and economic unit. India further more represents one of the oldest living civilizations of the world and has been the centre of culture for centuries.

" Yet India is to-day a dependency of Great Britain which is represented at this conference by the grace and by the agency of her imperial Government. She is without a national Government or a national flag and without any national representation or diplomatic exchange in the councils of nations except by employees and appointees of her British masters.

" Such a state of affairs, I submit is not only a grave moral and political wrong to India but a travesty of the claim that the United Nations' Conference consists of representatives of Sovereign nations. Continuance of such a situation affecting the honour, liberty, peace and progress of one-fifth of mankind is irreconcilable alike with the concepts that have inspired the United Nations' Conference and with the new world order which it is hoped will be ushered in as a result of its concrete decisions.

IMPERIALISM SHOULD GO

" Commissar Molotov has said " we all know that a time will come when the voice of independent India will be heard ", why should such voice not be heard now? The Indian National Congress party, representing the Indian people has always stood uncompromisingly against Fascism, Nazism and Imperialism. Organised Fascism and Nazism have now been liquidated. Imperialism alone remains and is entrenched in a system which implies coercion, domination and exploitation of one country by another. I submit that this system should be denounced in principle and abandoned in practice by an unequivocal acknowledgment and declaration of a free India.

" I speak here for my country because its national voice has been stilled by British duress. I also speak for those countries which are under the heels of alien militarists and cannot speak for themselves. I speak in particular for Burma, Malaya, Indo-China and Dutch East Indies, all bound to my own country by the closest ties of historical and cultural kinship and which cherish aspirations to national freedom like our own. Liberation from Japan should mean for them, I submit, liberation from all alien imperialism so far as this Conference is concerned.

" The voice of some 600 million enslaved people of Asia may not be officially heard at this Conference and those who have usurped their birthright and freedom may cynically claim to speak for them but there will be no real peace on this earth so long as they are denied justice. Recognition of India's independence now will be a proclamation and assurance to the whole world that the statement of the United Nations assembled at the solemn conclave at San Francisco have in truth and honour heralded the dawn of a new and better day for an all but crucified humanity."

During that period, Count Richard Kalergi of the New York University, also presented a memorandum on the San Francisco Conference to Mr. Stettinius, demanding that India be granted a permanent seat on the United Nations' Security Council.

The Memorandum was humane. The cause which it represented was not entertained by the Council of inhuman diplomats. The question of India's freedom was not included in the agenda of the Council. They had met at San Francisco solely with a view to discuss and debate and draw out a Charter for maintenance of peace in the world. They hoped for peace in the world while 400 million souls of India were in the shackles of slavery. Yet they had the guts to say that the question of India's freedom did not fall within the purview of this discussion.

The patriotic Indians in America tried to raise the question of India's present status and future freedom at many press conferences. Mr. Singh put the question to Messrs. Stettinius, Stassen and Vendenberg of the American delegation, Mr. Evait of Australia, Mr. Soong of China, Romulo of Phillipines, Mr. Attlee and Lord Cranborne of the British delegation. Most of the answers were evasive. Mr. Stassen, the spokesman of the American delegation, was straightforward. He made it clear that there were specific territories which were not to be discusssed in connection with trusteeship. Neither was the Independence of India to be a conference matter. In the light of what Mr. Stassen said the memorandum submitted by Mrs. Vijaya Lakshmi remained just a piece of information. The diplomats refused to discuss it. Some of the delegates expressed the view that India could present her case to the New League of Nations when and if one came into existence. This is how powerful nations hush up the weaker ones.

Mrs. Vijaya Lakshmi Pandit deserves her countrymen's gratitude. She presented our case to the San Francisco Conference. She exposed credentials of the so-called Defenders of Freedom and Democracy ".

Presentation of a memorandum to the world security conference was worth while. Advocating India's right to Self-Government and freedom was worth the sacrifice. It formed the major part of her pogramme in America. She carried on a single-handed campaign throughout the length and breadth of the great continent. She acquainted the Americans with the state of affairs in India. She enlisted their sympathy for the cause of Indian freedom. One of the leading dailies of India observed :

" Reports of her public addresses have been sent to the Indian press and her private off the record discussions have been considered by Indian leaders to be of great value in explaining the Indian situation to prominent Americans."

At public gatherings she advocated the supreme necessity of releasing Indian leaders, who were rotting in jail.

Having been questioned as to what kind of India would emerge, should the British relinquish power, she said, "India wants a popular, democratic Government which will ensure to all Indians the enjoyment of the four freedoms enunciated by President Roosevelt. Under such a Government India would whole-heartedly co-operate with other freedom-loving nations to build a better and safer world."

Asked frequently whether the release of Congress Leaders would bring about disorder in India Mrs. Pandit emphatically retorted " No, that is just an excuse and not a very good one".

IV

LAKSHMI FLASHES FORTH

Fiery energetic Mrs. Vijaya-lakshmi Pandit, sister of Pt. Jawaharlal Nehru, since the beginning of the United Nations' Conference, has been conducting a "one-woman" campaign to bring the cause of India's freedom to the attention of the 'Frisco delegates, cables Reuter's special correspondent :—

> " Mrs. Pandit has been making full use of this opportunity, putting in seven days' hard work per week.
>
> " At 8 a.m. each day she is awakened by the ringing of the telephone—usually a press representative clamouring for an interview.
>
> " Time is fixed for that on an already-crowded appointment book and then Mrs. Pandit has her breakfast of coffee and orange juice while she goes through her morning mail and newspapers.
>
> " The mail is voluminous and usually comes from people who comment on her work, promise her support or ask for more information on the Indian nationalist movement.

"On many days, large bouquets and baskets of flowers and fruits arrive for her, usually from people she does not even know, but who have heard her talk or read about her in the press.

"There are 2,000 correspondents concentrated here to cover the Conference and hundreds have requested for a talk with her. She has been able to see nearly all of them by keeping a strict 15-minute interview schedule in which she tries to cover as much ground as possible.

"After lunch Mrs. Pandit usually takes a short walk through the city—shopping or seeing sights. She has become so well-known a figure recognisable by her white or black saries that citizens flock after her in streets to get her autograph or snap her picture. The other day, a crowd even ignored the Hollywood star, James Cagney, in a restaurant and trooped around her table to get her signature.

Lately, Mrs. Pandit has been visiting San Francisco China Town—largest Chinese settlement outside China. There going down its hilly main street, which, she says, reminds her of Chandni Chauk in Delhi, she looks at silken jades and other oriental objects. At present she is trying to buy a graduation present for her daughter Chandra Lekha who will finish her studies at Wellesley College in a few months.

"Later, Mrs. Pandit visits the Headquarters of the Indian National Committee where she finds more mail and more invitations to cocktail parties, dinners and public appearances. She answers phone calls, writes letters and, if necessary, dictates statements and press releases which are handed to correspondents immediately. Sometimes she arranges little receptions in her apartment.

"She has already entertained foreign ministers of Egypt, Iraq and Saudi Arabia. Her evenings are taken up with dinner engagements, radio or personal appearances and other public functions.

"Although her schedule is extremely heavy, Mrs. Pandit does her best to present the Indian nationalist cause to as many people as possible. Towards ten at night she returns home where more messages and letters and phone calls await her. After they are disposed of, she finally returns with a book and around midnight lights go out and everything is quiet—until the next day."

She made it clear that her campaign was not with a view to secure American help for India's deliverance. She believed that none could help India to win her freedom except her own people. She only wanted to show the Americans the other side of the picture. This side had been screened off by vile British propaganda. And with these objectives she put in seven days solid work in a week.

As early as 8 o'clock in the morning the telephone bell from some prospective visitor woke her up. In hurry she gulped in her morning coffee and orange juice, did her toilet, and thumbing through the morning papers for a few moments, would be up for her interviews.

During the days of the Conference there were thousands of press correspondents in San Francisco to cover the news. Hundreds of them requested her for a little talk and she met almost all of them.

During her stay over there she received a pretty heavy dak from friends and admirers ; she even received letters and gifts from persons who didn't know her personally, they had simply read about her activities in the press.

After lunch she would have a little walk. Sometimes she went for shopping. Thereafter again she reverted to interviews. She met President Truman and Lady Truman, entertained Foreign ministers of Egypt, Iraq and Saudi Arabia, and a host of other prominent visitors from different countries of the world. She presented India's case to as many people as possible

Her evenings were spent in dinner engagements, Radio or personal appearances, and other public functions. Most of the arrangements in connection with her radio talks, public lectures, etc., were made by Dr. Anup Singh, the Washington Representative of the National Committee for India, and Editor of the *Voice of India*. He went to California weeks before to make the necessary preparations.

V

ADDRESS TO CALIFORNIA LEGISLATURE

Beneath the gold dome of the capital building of Sacramento, capital of California, Mrs. Vijaya-laxmi Pandit declared that new ties forged between America and India would help the solution not only of India's problem, but the problem of colonial possessions everywhere, said, Stanley Burch Reuter's chief editor in America, in a radio despatch.

In an earnest speech calling for sympathy for India's campaign for independence, delivered at the invitation of the State Legislature, Mrs. Pandit told the Assembly men " So long as these colonial vested interests remain, there can be no peace, there can be no security. And so long as there is no security or peace, we shall go on destroying all that generations and centuries of human effort have built up. I believe these new ties will work for common good between peoples of the world—because it is the people who are going to build up the world structure."

The legislature of California sitting in the city which was the centre of the famous gold rush of 1849 adjourned a debate on the State's budget to hear Mrs. Pandit. They sat at the back of rows of desks littered with financial papers to hear her eloquent speech.

ONE UNITY

Declaring, that the world must not think in terms of national freedom, but of the freedom for the whole world, Mrs. Pandit said : " We must inevitably consider America and India and all nations of the world as one unity. Therefore, I am happy to be able to tell you that in India we have come closer to America in understanding through those men who to-day are fighting in India. We have given them welcome and we believe they have brought back to America memories of friendship and understanding.

" No question can be solved by itself. Unless we are prepared to accept certain principles, we shall not be successful, however hard we try to find a solution to the problem of permanent peace and the security of the world."

TIES OF CULTURAL CONTACTS

" In this reconstruction it is necessary to have the help and friendship of all nations. It is necessary to build up a new world with ties of cultural contacts, industrial and commercial contacts and contacts of every sort.

" Before we can talk about interdependence, we must realise that it is only through independence that we can achieve interdependence. Because, I feel that so strongly, that I must remind you that if India were to-day an independent country, she would throw in her weight to a much larger measure and would help in building up the structure of security and permanent peace which is the aim of the nations at San Francisco.

" India has it in her heart to work with other nations to help in an organisation of the world in which all people can live in honour and justice. To a degree to which justice is denied to any group of people, to that degree will all these conferences have failed and the structure that has been envisaged for permanent peace be a failure also.

" So long as we think in terms of power politics and political expediency, we cannot hope to achieve anything of lasting value. But if the foundations of the new world structure are laid on justice and on the recognition of independence of all peoples, I believe it will be possible to avoid future conflicts and to have a world in which all people can work together for common good.

" It is not only a question of recognition of the principle of ultimate independence. The resolution has to be translated into action. I would like you in America to understand how vital it is for the future of the world that these problems are approached in terms of realism and understanding and that this independence—which is something so dear to you, which you have fought to preserve—is something which those, who have not yet achieved it, value even more dearly than you who now possess it."

" Declaring that the people of India tremendously admired the people of England, Mrs. Pandit said that it was the system they fought, not the people. Only with the liquidation of the system of Colonial domination could there be any harmony in the world.

THE FUTURE

Mrs. Pandit concluded her reaffirmation of her belief in the future which the world could built up. "I believe the future will be built up into a really beautiful thing through the efforts of all those who desire justice, honour and peace among nations.

"I think America is going to play a vital part in this new world structure. But you cannot hold on to your greatness, unless you realise, that it is by sharing and not by possessing, that the world rises. The extent to which you insist on this principle will be the extent to which you have achieved greatness now and in the world to come."

Mr. Ernest Debs, the Assembly man who took a leading part in inviting Mrs. Pandit and who presided over the house, thanked her for the speech with the declaration that "a hundred and fifty years ago we in the United States were striving for the same thing which you are striving for. I feel strongly on the subject of freedom not only for India but for all peoples all over the world."

When it was announced that Mrs. Pandit had been invited to address the legislature, a number of Assembly men sought to have the speech indefinitely postponed on the grounds that they had not the time for further interruption on the budget debate.

Mr. Debs took the lead in blocking this resolution and today when the session opened the Speaker, Mr. Charles Lyon withdrew to let Mr Debs take the chair.

The invitation to Mrs. Pandit followed a number of addresses she had made to women's groups in Sacramento, outspokenly attacking the Indian delegation to the San Francisco Conference as unrepresentative of the Indian people. There was a full House to hear her speech, but the assembly men sat in silence not applauding her until the end of the address.

VI

VISIT TO BALTIMORE

A report of her visit to Baltimore was published in the *Tribune*, dated 10th April 1945. America in general heartfully reacted to her speeches :—

" The visit of Mrs. Pandit who lectured in the City's largest auditorium, resulted in new social relationships between the whites and the Negroes as well as lively political talk about India."

Mrs. Pandit's visit received the highest official recognition. The City's Mayor welcomed her at the railway station and presented " Keys of the City ." These are traditionally reserved for the most notable guests.

In her lecture arranged at the theatre, thirty per cent of the audience consisted of Negroes besides Indians, Chinese, Japanese and Americans. Mrs. Pandit said that India stood for equality of all peoples and races. India was entirely sympathetic with the U. S. Negroes. This aroused a great ovation. Next day a leading American Newspaper headlined the lecture:

" India stands for equality," says Mrs. Pandit. Mrs. Juantia Mitchell, President of the Baltimore section of the National Association for the advancement of coloured people said that the coloured people in America were cent per cent behind the Indian freedom movement.

VII

SHE SPEAKS TO SIKHS

Mr. Vijaya Lakshmi Pandit spent Sunday among some 5,000 Sikhs near San Francisco, explaining to them the meaning of the United Nations' Conference, cabled Reuter's special correspondent in America from Stockton, California on May 15, 1945.

Addressing thousands who had come from all parts of California where they are now settled, Mrs. Pandit spoke from the dais in the famous Stockton Sikh temple, which is the only building of its kind in the United States. She said : " My memory here goes back to the days enveloped in the dark clouds of oppression--when somany in India had to undergo so much suffering and sorrow. The situation is somewhat better now, but still we are not free. We are going on with the fight, not only for the cause of India, but for the cause of freedom of oppressed people everywhere."

Addressing herself directly to hundreds of Americans among the audience, she declared : " Our fight is much bigger than the fight for freedom of just one people. It is a fight for a world-wide freedom. You Americans have been watching San Francisco and hoping that from this conference will come a just and lasting peace. But it cannot be a success when the people who are there claim to settle the destiny of the world without first consulting the wishes of the people of the world. For us—who are outside the conference—it is very important to draw the attention of the delegates to the principles of right and justice on which a lasting peace must be built. Our leaders forget when deciding on important issues that personal freedom is one of the most important concepts upon which world peace is founded.

Today, we cannot afford to make any more mistakes in planning the future of mankind. We made some grave mistakes after the last war and endured unheard of miseries and sufferings. Today, the world cannot endure any more suffering. This time we have to decide to make good the mistakes made after the last war.

Only through the freedom of India can we contribute to the freedom of the rest of the world.

" We are rejoicing today in the defeat of Fascism, but we forget the cause of Fascism—Imperialism.

"Unless that is defeated too, there can be no peace in the world, no matter how many San Francisco Conferences we hold. We must raise our voice to say that peace must be based on the fundamental principles of democracy—unless the Allies of today split up to become the enemies of to-morrow."

Mrs. Pandit who motored with newsmen and members of her party from San Francisco to Stockton was received by the whole Sikh community and the Mayor of the town.

VIII

WHO REPRESENTS INDIA ?

The well-known American journalist Bruce Bliven, in an article contributed to the " New Republic " on the India question " being shouldered aside " said on May 10, 1945 :—

" India is only represented by the brilliant and beautiful Mrs. Pandit and able journalists ' who rise at every press conference to ask forbidden questions.' "

For sometime during her stay in America she put up in a hotel where Sir Feroze and other delegates to the San Francisco Conference were staying. Sir Feroze Khan Noon invited her to tea. She however declined to accept the invitation, telling Sir Feroze that they had come to America on diametrically opposite "missions." He was an agent of British Imperialism. She was an advocate of a subject people. There was no common ground between them for meeting.

IX

INDIA THANKS LAKSHMI

The late Mr. Kalinath Ray wrote the same remarkable editorial on Mrs. Vijaya Lakshmi Pandit's activities in America :—

"A Tory publicist openly cursed Mrs. Vijayalakshmi Pandit the other day. In doing so he revealed what emotions were surging in the hearts of British Conservatives. Messrs. Churchill & Co. could not but feel distressed and nettled at the systematic pricking of their anti-Indian propaganda bubbles in the United States by Mrs. Vijayalakshmi Pandit. It was argued on behalf of British Imperialism that by delivering political speeches in America she was violating the undertaking given by her to the Government to the effect that while she was abroad, she would keep her lips sealed. Mrs. Vijayalakshmi Pandit has in a press statement issued by her at San Francisco denied the existence of any such undertaking. Undoubtedly the primary object of her visit to the United States was to see her two daughters and arrange for the education of the third. But that did not mean that she would be a mute spectator of Imperialist agents' and hirelings' activities which were clearly calculated to cause a serious injury to the interests of India. Several lies had been made current in America. For instance, it had been repeatedly declared that Mahatma Gandhi and the Congress were pro-Japanese. Again it had been repeatedly proclaimed that India was no better than a house divided against itself. These blatant lies had to be nailed to the counter.

And if Mrs. Vijayalakshmi Pandit nailed them to the counter she committed no crime or sin. It is certainly not her fault that her captivating personality attracts large American audiences who invariably listen to her with rapt attention. She does not mince matters. She is in the habit of calling a spade a spade. That is what the people of the United States like the most. Now Mrs. Vijayalakshmi Pandit is at San Francisco. Her presenee there must be giving the "Indian delegation" sleepless nights. She has already fired the first shot. This is what she has declared :

'I desire to make it clear that the so-called Indian representatives attending the San Francisco Conference have not the slightest representative capacity, no sanction and no mandate from any of the responsible groups in India and are merely nominees of the British Government. Anything they say here or any vote they cast can have no binding effect or force on the people of India.' These so-called Indian representatives are themselves conscious of the fact that they are British Imperialism's puppets. They do not venture to make public utterances and face critical international journalists. According to a United Press of America message 'they seldom leave the hotel' in which they are staying and 'often eat in their rooms.' Perhaps the presumption that they are more ashamed of their unrepresentative character than tired will not be wrong. Referring to these 'representatives' of the 'great captive power, India' Mr. Iftone, 'P. M.'s' correspondent, says: 'They have been chosen by the Government without consultation of Indian parties or political leaders, most of whom are still in jail, including the far-seeing Nehru who would have shone even in a gathering of giants.' When Pt. Jawaharlal Nehru's sister addresses the press conference, which she intends to call shortly, the atmosphere at San Francisco will become too hot for Messrs. Noon & Co."

X

INDIA'S CHARMING WOMAN.

The following tribute was paid to Mrs. Pandit in London on Oct. 8, 1945 :—

The great part Indian women will play in assisting India to independence and afterwards was stressed by Mrs. Casey, wife of Mr. R. G. Casey, Governor of Bengal, in an interview.

The future of the women of India is very bright, she said. People like Mrs. Sarojini Naidu and Mrs. Vijayalakshmi

Pandit have set a great example to the rest of Indian women and, if this example is followed, women will accept more and more responsibility in the national life. There is a realisation in India that women have a part to play, instead of being kept in seclusion. Indian women are both charming and highly intelligent as well as unboring.

"I believe in entry to public life of more and more women because women have far more to learn than men in these matters and are usually more realists."

Mrs. Casey turned to India's needs for the future :—

"While I cannot speak with authority about India as a whole, I feel that the greatest problems facing Bengal are those of irrigational communications and education," she said.

"It would be a difficult job to popularise birth-control in a country like India, where religion is so powerful, but, if the people are decently fed and educated, experience tends to the view that they might limit the families without artificial aids."

An appeal to Indians to concern themselves with practical rather than academic matters, in order to fit themselves for self-Government, was made by Mrs. Casey.

XI

MISS PANDIT ADDRESSES MISS AMERICA

In the footsteps of her mother Miss Chandra Lekha delivered a vigorous speech at New York on October 11, 1945.

Twenty-one years old, Chandra Lekha Pandit, elder daughter of Mrs. Vijaya Lakshmi Pandit, was given an ovation when she addressed a meeting of the East and West Association on the question of "what is the fundamental right for a people to be really themselves."

Miss Pandit represented India in the discussions in which youthful speakers from other countries participated.

She said a major fundamental right which the people of India must have in order to be really themselves is the right to govern themselves. It was only after this freedom was ours and a National Government represented the citizens, that the people of India could gain many other rights which were necessary for their well-being such as the right to education and medical care, the right of assembly and the right to read, write and speak freely. The four freedoms had been one of the most popular war slogans, but because these freedoms were not clearly defined and were not applicable to the whole world, there had been global unrest since the end of the war.

Miss Pandit continued: "In Asia the recent disturbances in Java and Indo-China serve to point out that the new world order cannot be based on the pattern of slavery followed in the past. Because India, with her vast natural resources and cultural heritage, has much to contribute to the world of to-day and because Indians constitute one-fifth of the human race, the future of India will influence the whole of Asia. The Indian cultural pattern is based on the ideal of service for humanity. The old Sanskrit proverb is 'individual for family—family for community—community for nation and nation for the world.' History has proved that the Indian people have lived up time and again to this concept and their contribution to the cause of world peace and security can be a most valuable one, but it can only come if, in the words of our leader, Mr. Gandhi, they have the freedom."

XII

ATOMIC IMPERIALISM

"Not the atomic bomb but greater explosives of greed and imperialism threaten the world today," said Mrs.

Vijaya Lakshmi Pandit, sister of Pt. Jawaharlal Nehru in a broadcast talk.

She added : " The United States has emerged to the special position of leadership in Asia—a position of grave moral responsibility in the eyes of Asiatic people. From one end of the continent to the other Asiatic peoples are in revolt against imperialism, exploitation and domination, but the British, French and Dutch are equally engaged in a cynical race to perpetuate serfdom and slavery.

" The spirit of revolt sweeping Indonesia, Indo-China, India, Burma, Iran, Palestine and Egypt is too wide and deep to be crushed by mere brute force. There will be no peace in Asia until the peoples have won their freedom."

XIII
THE ACID TEST

India will be the acid test of all that has been said regarding the moral issues of this war, declared Mrs. Vijayalaxmi Pandit in a speech. She said :

" In the freedom of India lies the hope of a settlement of the world problem. Free India becomes a force for good in the East and the whole problem of the Pacific becomes more easy of solution. A discontented India means a discontented Asia. There can be no lasting peace unless it is based on the recognition of human rights. The first step in this direction is the freedom of those countries still under foreign domination. Unless this is done, the present global conflict becomes merely a war for power with no moral sanction behind it. Statements are not enough. Good intentions do not go very far. It is only actions that will help in clarifying the issues and so far no such action has been taken by the United Nations. If the plan for post-war world is to concentrate on power and to impose systems of security on weaker nations, it is bound to fail. Civilisation is not a monopoly of the white man. Asia and Africa have a heritage which stretches far back into antiquity and the world is as much in need of a message of these great continents as any that Europe and America have to give."

XIV

GOODBYE, UNCLE SHAM!

Having floored the enemies of India in America, Mrs. Vijiaya Lakshmi Pandit returned to her motherland as a heroine. India's great Ambassador to America returned home towards the end of January 1946 and landed at the American Airbase Drigh Road, Karachi. She was profusely garlanded immediately on landing of the plane.

In spite of a very warm reception accorded to Mrs. Pandit everywhere in America, she does not believe in Uncle Sham's professions of international democracy. America is playing Britain's game and therefore she will not let her countrymen be misled by illusions of sympathy from America. India must depend on the strength of her own arms.

If we cannot achieve our freedom, America will not help us to achieve it. That is the golden lesson of the whirlwind tour undertaken by Vijaya Lakshmi in America. Uncle Sham is cultivating industrial imperialism which is as dangerous as Britain's political imperialism, John Bull and Uncle Sham are now thick as thieves. And India can expect but little from a gang of robbers.

CHAPTER ELEVENTH

The Princess Charming

In the name of the Eternal,
In the name of the Master of Strength,
In the name of Him who moves not !
Wayfarer in this place,
Look not upon the glass of appearance,
For a breath may shatter it
And illusion is a pit for the feet of men.

—TUNADIR AL'KHANSA

(Translated from the Arabian by E. Powys Mathers)

Sweet Swarup !—Lovely Lakshmi !—Precious Pandit ! There is hardly an adjective that will not fittingly adorn our beauteous Vijaya Lakshmi. And her charm is not merely of the body but also of the soul. In spite of her feminine fascinations, she worships the Master of Strength. In spite of her abounding charms, Mrs. Vijaya Lakshmi Pandit is not a slave of the looking glass. She knows that beauty is an illusion. And illusion is a pit for the feet of men.

I

LANGUAGE OF BEAUTY

The dictionary definition of beauty is this: "Combination of qualities, as shape, proportion, colour, in human face or form, or in other objects, that delight the sight." It is worth while to consider the views of poets and writers about beauty :—

And beautiful as sweet !
And young as beautiful ! And soft as young !

And gay as soft! And innocent as gay!—*Rev. E. Young.*

*   *   *   *

For she] was beautiful; her beauty made,
The bright world dim, and everything beside
Seemed like the fleeting image of a shade.—*Shelley.*

*   *   *   *

As rich and purposeless as is the rose.
Thy simple doom is to be beautiful.—*Stephen Philips.*

*   *   *   *

The saying that beauty is but skin-deep is a skin-deep saying—*Herbert Spencer.*

*   *   *   *

It is an extremely wretched thing to be over-handsome.—*Plautus.*

*   *   *   *

Thou hast no faults, or I no faults can spy,
Thou art all beauty, or all blindness I.—*Christopher Codrington.*

*   *   *   *

And lightly was her slender nose,
Tip-tilted like the petal of a flower.—*Tennyson.*

*   *   *   *

O, that her hand,
In whose comparison all whites are ink,
Writing their own reproach, to whose soft seizure,

*   *   *   *

The cygnet's down is harsh.—*Shakespeare.*

*   *   *   *

And sweet, red, splendid kissing mouth.—*Swinburne.*

*   *   *   *

The dew that on the violet lies
Mocks the dark lustre of thine eyes.--*Scott.*

*   *   *   *

The flowers anew returning seasons bring,
Beauty, faded, has no second spring.—*Ambrose Phillips.*

*   *   *   *

A daughter of the gods, divinely tall,
And most divinely fair.—*Tennyson.*

*   *   *   *

Beauty is the flower of virtue.—*Proverb.*

* * * *

I would that you were either less beautiful or less corrupt. Such perfect beauty does not suit such imperfect morals.—*Ovid.*

* * * *

Beauty stands
n th' admiration only of weak minds
I ed captive.—*Milton.*

* * * *

Her angel's face
As the great eye of heaven, shyned bright
And made a sunshine in the shady place;
Did never mortal eye behold such heavenly grace?—*Spenser.*

* * * *

Thus it is clear that beauty is not necessarily what the people usually understand by it. The definition of Rev. F. Young is applicable to Vijaya Lakshmi. She is sweet as beautiful, young as sweet, soft as young, gay as soft, and innocent as gay. Her beauty does not make everything dim, as Shelley would have it, but everything beside her does seem like the fleeting image of a shade, because no paints and powders can stand the force of her outpourings. She is rich in beauty, in the terms of Stephen Philips, but she is certainly not purposeless like the rose and her simple doom is not to be beautiful but also to beautify others. Some people think that beauty is skin-deep, but skin-deep (in the language of Herbert Spencer) is certainly a skin-deep saying so far as it applies to Vijaya Lakshmi, because her beauty is heart-deep and even goes as far as her soul.

If it is an extremely wretched thing to be over-handsome, as stated Plautus, Vijaya Lakshmi has nothing to be sorry for, because she is certainly not over-handsome. Christopher Codrington's dictum did apply to her when Ranjit crossed many bridges to win her love. He certainly could not find any fault in her. There is no doubt that at that time her nose (in the Tennysonian verbiage) was tip-tilted like the petal of a flower.

Shakespeare is too hyperbolic to be true, but Swinburne might have found her lips sweet, red and splendid. Scott might have realised that the dew on the violet twenty years ago did imitate the lustre of her eyes. If flowers are born in the spring (if that be the argument of Ambrose Phillips), the flowers of Lakshmi's spirit are blooming even in autumn. Had Tennyson been alive, he would have agreed with me that Vijaya Lakshmi is the daughter of the gods, divinely tall and most divinely fair. If beauty is the flower of virtue, as says a proverb, Lakshmi has plenty of these flowers. Ovid need not worry himself to another death in his ancient grave, beacuse the perfect beauty of Vijaya Lakshmi suits her perfect morals perfectly. We may not agree with Milton of the Puritan age, because we live in the twentieth century, that beauty stands in the admiration of the weak minds led captive.

Let Spenser be satisfied in heaven that Lakshmi's angelic eye shines bright as the great eye of heaven. She makes a sunshine in the shady place. Her cheerful spirit lit up even the dull and drowsy office in the U. P. secretariat. The speech delivered by her at the Allahabad Culture Centre on March 29, 1946 brings out the beauty of her spirit and her mission of life.

"When freedom is so near, we must see to the freedom of our own home and freedom of our society." Thus observed Mrs. Vijaya Lakshmi Pandit in opening the Home Decoration Exhibition in the Besant Hall organised by the Allahabad Culture Centre.

Mrs. Pandit added that at the present time they were half-Anglicised and could not get freedom unless their society and their houses got freedom. They should not forget that

India has a rich heritage of culture and art and they should strive to bring them back to their pristine glory. She pointed out that proportion and symmetry were lacking in Indian homes. One thing they should bear in mind was that Art could unite both East and West. Education in Fine Art was a very useful thing and especially girls must derive great benefit from it. Education could not be said to be complete by merely taking degrees in Universities or by beautifying their bodies. But they should look to their houses and beautify them. They should be enthusiastic for this kind of art. The younger generation, especially the girls, should take interest in beautifying their homes.

II

LOVELY LADY LAKSHMI

Vijaya Lakshmi Pandit, in her life, combines all that is best in the East and the West. One finds in her person the 'red enamel caste mark' on her forehead and the ' scarlet lacquered finger and toe nails', pleasantly harmonised into a charming individuality.

She has all the manners and etiquettes of a modern American belle. But her heart throbs with the Kashmiri Brahmin blood. Her ancestor, Raj Kaul, who founded the family gained eminence in the court of Farrukhsiar as a scholar of Sanskrit and Persian.

She relishes no doubt the breezy free mode of living in the West. She has in her own manner adopted traits of European life. She loves to use a fork and a knife on the dinner table. Instead of bending, she shakes hands with a European visitor. She would shake her head with disgust at the sight of a woman ' rickety and emaciated,' wrapped in Pardah, walking measured steps behind her 'Lord' in matrimony. The purdah and the caste give her nausea. These are all the lingering snakes of the Eastern Civilization. She has no respect for them. These are relics of barbarism. Their days are numbered.

On the other hand, other however, she is not unconscious of the dangers of blindly aping the European modes of life.

" Having lost the power of free thought, we have become hypnotised by catchwords from the West and have fashioned our lives according to them." Thus she warns us against a harmful transplanation of inadjustable Western modes of life in the Indian soil.

" We have our own great heritage, and while combining with it whatever may be of use and value and beauty from the West, the fundamental must be of the East lone." She said in an address delivered at J. T. H. School Allahabad, on Feb., 25, 1939.

Vijaya Lakshmi has exquisitely combined the beauty of the East and the West in her personality. She has little faith in make-up. Sarojini Naidu recently declared that she uses lipstick on her forehead. That is certainly the Indian way. Lakshmi, of course does not go so far. When she does encourage make-up, it is only the 'natural' make-up that she advocates. It is worth while to distinguish "Natural Make-up" from the " Extreme Smart " beautification :—

There are two major types of beauty accentuation which are currently popular. One is the "natural" style, the other, the "smart extreme."

The "Natural" type offers an artistically restrained accentuation of all naturally apparent beauty features through the various mediums offered by cosmetics, costumes and coiffure.

" Extreme Smart " beautification presents an exaggeration of natural features, or the creation of feature effects which actually are not existing. The natural make-up type is the best for nearly all women. In about 9 cases out of 10, feminine good looks are much more completely and surely flattered by the "Natural" type than by the "extreme smart." Very young women should not go in for extreme make-up effects. It makes women in their teens or twenties look older, and thus completely blot out the most striking beauty of all, that of youth. Don't even experiment with such "smart-extreme" make-up unless you have passed thirty. From this age on such make-up generally doesn't seem to either add or detract from one's years.

If you haven't ventured into the smart extremes of make-up, don't think that you must. The odds are that such a move wouldn't add to you glamour. But, if you have been favouring the extreme in make-up stylish, you should experiment with returning to the "Natural" style of beauty accenturation. (Condensed from an article by Max Facter Jr. famous make-up adviser to screen stars).

III

DAUGHTERS OF INDIA

Lakshmi's conception of a woman is rather manful. She never thinks of her as the weaker vessel. She does not like a girl " who sits on a cushion and sews a fine seam." There is no use feeding upon strawberries, sugar and butter.

She thinks that 'the strawberries are beginning to pall, and too much cream and sugar are bad for the digestion'. Sex-equality sums up her view-point regarding the relationship between man and woman in life. She not merely preaches complete equality between man and woman. Her life is a practical example of the "purdahless" philosophy.

She does not have any traditional reverence for the repressive social laws of society. These have kept women in bondage. She would not take them as 'absolute and final writs of providence'. She calls a spade a spade. Necessary and natural, without fear of contradiction, she attacks the so-called defenders of the masculine faith. Tracing the back-ground of the subjection of women she observed :

" We (women) in the East are even to-day hedged in by taboos of various description .... the very system of female education was designed with the idea of persuading woman that she was in need of protection which could be given only if she would abide by certain rules. In no period of her existence has woman been free."

From a general survey of the back-ground of social man-over-woman superiority in the world, she passes on to Indian conditions. She gives a fleeting thought to the social laws of Manu, the great Law-giver of the Hindu India in ancient days. His verdicts are still acted upon in the form of provisions in the modern Hindu law. His anti-women views are widely respected by the orthodox folk. There is no doubt that ancient sages in Hinduism, laid down great truths pregnant with valuable wisdom. These were based upon intensive experience of men and matters ; but they have also formulated principles which in the present times cannot command respect from people with democratic and scientific views. Some of these principles had their social value when they were formulated. The changed social environments need relaxation. Apart from them, there are customs and traditions which were unjust even at the time when they were enacted. They were somehow accepted by the ancient people. The social philosophy of that time was less evolved. The 'aggressor' and the 'possessor' in man governed their social outlook. It may be said that the aggressor and the possessor in man is still there. But it has drifted to other channels of social activity. It is relaxing its stranglehold on relationship between the sexes.

Mrs. Vijaya Lakshmi Pandit's social view-point leads to a general discussion of a principle which is so vital to women. Mrs. Vijaya Lakshmi Pandit's view-point regarding our religious laws, beautifully illuminates the relationship between men and women. Referring to the laws of Manu, in the course of the radio talk, she said :

" In our own country the famous law-giver Manu, has expressed the same sentiment. According to him a woman in childhood must be protected by her father, in youth by her husband, in old age by her son, and I am tempted to add that all times by her priest, for perhaps nowhere more than in India is woman the unconscious victim of the priest." How bold is she ! In an ultra-religious country like India, dogma holds its sway over the masses in all spheres of life. Even a statesman in order to win over the following of the masses has to become 'half priest—half politician.' It is risky to trespass the domain of the priest. But what does she care ? She has respect for the finer and fuller principles of life. These alone for her constitute the spirit of religion. She like other rationalists of to-day, interprets religion in terms of social relations. (With a rational and inquisitive mind she wonders if there can be any other interpretation of the traditional religion).

The subjection of Indian women, however, doesn't end with the priest. To maintain this grip upon the ignorant folks, the priest must have a noose. The upkeep of the system requires a class of supporters or pillars. The system is the dogmatic way of life. It is exhibited in the caste, and the clan. The pillars of the system consist of generally the old men and women, who too like the priest have their own spheres of authority over the youngmen and women. She says :

" Brought up in the four walls of her house the Indian girl was the property of her father, who gave her away in marriage. She then became the property of her husband and her whole life was spent in humble and devoted service. If she would have the misfortune to become a widow, she bowed in submission to her sons. Religion, caste and society laid down certain rules, which had to be observed in order to secure protection for the woman and ensure happiness and prosperity for her husband's family. If she swerved from this path, she became an out-caste. This duty was in almost every instance, defined by man, but ruthlessly enforced by the older women, who have spent their lives in independence and subjection. They were not going to allow their grand daughters the freedom, which had been withheld from them, and so, as slaves have always done, it was the older women of the family and the community who enforced discipline." This is an excellent heart-to-heart talk to young girls. She is not against old women in their individual capacities. On the contrary she loved them in her own family. She has all possible regard for them. What she hates is the system. The younger generations must not be kept under ruthless subordination to the older men and women. The erroneous philosophy of life which has evolved this faulty system must go.

It is worth while to compare the ideas of Lakshmi Pandit with those of Sarojini Naidu speaking in Calcutta in a different context. We find that immoral traffic, due to contact with the West, is constantly on the increase. While on one hand we have to save ourselves from the evils of the East, we have also to guard ourselves from the gripping evils of the West.

" Your women are to you the flower of the spring-time and hopes of the future. They are to you the source of inspiration and mirth and happiness. I, therefore, charge you to stamp out the evil of immoral traffic in women and build up a new world in which a man and woman can live equally with high hopes and in which no man shall dare to spoil the sanctity of women," said Mrs. Sarojini Naidu addressing a mammoth meeting held at the Calcutta University Institute Hall under the joint auspices of several organisations.

Mrs. Naidu said: " It is an immemorial and universal vice that civilisation has brought with it. And to-day the new civilisation of which we all boast so much has without diminishing the inequity of its tradition multiplied a thousand-fold.

" I remember when I was a child I used to see pictures which I did not understand at that time which were of beautiful slaves being sold in Rome and Babylon and men looking at them. It was a sale in commodity of human flesh. That is taking place to-day only rather more decently and more openly. Fierce epidemic of anger was passing through Europe because of the white slave traffic in which were involved not girls of Bengal but white girls, English, French, German and others who used to be lured away for promises of some gain—all educated white girls—and ultimately to be taken away and sold to brothels in South America. But in our country unfortunately the social code has been rather relaxed for many centuries in particular matters. "

Continuing she said: " Our women must be part of beauty. And that beauty of women born of purity that Sita and Savitri gave to us that women would be dishonoured by the husband, by the son, by the brother who went to another woman who might otherwise have remained pure. In China, in Japan, in Asia it has been considered as a custom. Why call it a custom. Would a man dare to enter my house, where there is woman born of purity. That is morality. Remember that every woman that is victimised by you or your brother is bringing daily degradation to every other woman. Womanhood is one and indivisible and no woman whether she remains in pardah or comes out of the pardah for progressive works and say " My garment is clean ' while there is a stain on the garment of her sister. She too is unclean. This is the consciousness that is to be created throughout the country.

" Not a single woman be made victim of man's lust. No woman in India is chaste because we cannot separate ourselves from our sisters, who are unchaste. And on whom the burden falls ? On you. That is why I am so happy to see that men have come here in large numbers. If you say we will not tolerate the brothels, we will not sell the womanhood. We shall be the protectors, only then there can be a solution to this problem. My appeal is not to the women. They will do their duty. But you are the active co-operators in vice. (I do not mean you, but men who are co-operators in vice). It is, therefore, your duty to see that such an evil is wiped out from our midst. Do you like that thousands of our girls whom men have deserted for hunger and misery should be taken away like cattle for vile objects ? Do you like to feel that men, foreign men, who have come here for their own purposes of trade, of war, whatever it may be, are able to buy our women. If not, see to it that this custom which has grown so horribly in Bengal owing to the famine will be stamped out and each of you will become a champion of an unknown woman. "

Lord Bishop who opened the discussion of the meeting said that he was deeply interested in the subject to be discussed at the meeting, namely, immoral traffic in woman and children, since it was one of those on which the welfare of the country in which his life has been spent depended.

There is no evil, he said, which is more destructive to human character, and of social life. The very term 'immoral traffic' speaks to us the evil it connotes. It was inconceivable to modern thought.

Dr. Syamaprasad Mukherjee said : The problem was intimately connected with our national problem. There should be vigilent public opinion—relentless public opinion—to eradicate the social evil. Only Government legislations and public powers could do nothing.

Begum Shamsher Nahar moved the following resolution : "This public meeting of the citizens of Calcutta views with grave alarm the unprecedented increase in the traffic in women and children. It feels that advantage is being taken of the helplessness of women due to economic distress and emphatically condemns such exploitation. It urges that (a) Government should take immediate and adequate steps for the protection and rehabilitation of women by firm action ; (b) the Bengal suppression of Immoral Traffic Act be suitably amended to make its provisions really effective and capable of checking the evil."

Dr. Sourin Ghosh supporting the resolution disclosed that the number of prostitutes in Calcutta were in 1921—10,207 : in 1925—19,220, in 1938—22,000, and in 1944 over 45,000. He also disclosed that the Governor of Bengal on his own initiative has ordered to close down all brothels in Calcutta and from 15th December, about 60 brothels have been closed. He appealed to the citizens to see that the traffickers in brothels do not get any opportunity to open new brothels elsewhere.

In placing the resolution before the house for voting Mrs. Sarojini Naidu said : "In voting the resolution what I should ask you to remember to see is your imperative responsibility that the spirit of the resolution is honoured. You are also implicated in the duty of seeing that immoral traffic in women and children is abolished from our midst."

IV

THAT PICTURE—AND THIS

East has its own contribution to make to the Civilization of the world. The contribution of faith, love and sacrifice are the very fundamentals of the Eastern Philosophy of life. She admires the East. But there is a 'cancer in the heart of the rose.' And she is painfully conscious of the lurking adder.

She once got a chance to pay a visit to Hardwar at the time of the Kumbh Mela. The Hindus from every corner of India assembled at the place. The social intercourse which ensued in the 'babbling' of various tongues amused her. The banks of the holy Ganges, and transparent flow of water, and the pleasant climate, refreshed her mind, but she was distressed at the sight of religious demonstrations of the savage days. The marching of nude Sadhus in procession rankled in her mind.

While coming back she heard a journalist talking about these Sadhu demonstrations and denouncing them with vehemence :

"It was the most disgusting sight I have ever seen. ....these great vulgar men marching nude through the streets of Hardwar without any religious motive—just showing themselves off, making suggestive gestures—marching in a brazen manner, thwarting the authorities in the knowledge that they were supported by thousands of the ignorant to whom their flaunted nudity was a symbol of sainthood and the women ....old and young, rich and poor, throwing themselves at the feet of these rascals, fighting with each other, pushing each other in a desperate effort to touch the feet and receive the blessing of these holiest of Sadhus "

She conveyed it to the journalist, what she herself wanted to say. That was courageous on her part. In India people are most fussy and fanatic with regard to matters concerning religion. If a responsible person of her status forthright condemned the religious ceremonies, people would retort, recoil and protest. She herself felt what the journalist spoke out. Social evils and religious lapses are a dirty stigma on the name of Eastern Civilization. It is time we had discarded them. The sooner, the better. While going back from the Kumbh Mela, she ruminated over the sad plight of Indian masses, as witnessed in the course of the mela :

" I saw before me an enslaved people, poverty-stricken and down-trodden—their weak undeveloped bodies being a correct outer shell for their weak and undisciplined minds. —That India should have so fallen ! The land of beauty and courage, whose every corner was active even to-day with memories of beautiful deeds bravely done...whose sons had in the past considered death preferable to dishonour, whose fighters had upheld all those noble traditions which enabled India to survive through theages. To-day India was a land divided where brother fought against brother......"

V

IDEALS FOR INDIAN WOMEN

It is clear that we can neither run away from the East, nor can we find a comfortable shelter in the orchards of the West. We must adopt our culture to new modes of life and give what we cannot adopt and borrow from abroad what we do not find here. With that view Mrs. Vijaya Lakshmi Pandit is fully in agreement. Up to this time the ladies of India suffered from an inferiority complex so far as dress is concerned. But now we have come to realize that the Indian dress is far superior to the gowns and pants of the West now adopted by ladies in Europe and America.

The craze of wearing salwar and khameej—the dress of the Punjabi girls—is spreading like wild fire among the modern girls of Bombay and Sind.

This dress which has become inter-provincial and inter-communal was originally worn by the Muslim ladies. Only their khameej was very loose and reached almost their ankles, while the girls these days prefer their shirts to be more fitting and not quite so long.

If you ask a non-Punjabi girl why she wears a salwar and khameej, she might answer that because it happens to be the fashion. But besides being in fashion, it is a very comfortable dress and suits almost everybody. As our Indian girls don't like to exhibit their million dollar legs, the salwar forms a perfect covering for the legs. Girls who are tom-boyish and don't feel at home in sarees find the salwar jus to their taste.

In the heat of summer, instead of tying a saree, which is about five or sometimes six yards long, round one's self, it is better to wear a salwar which is much lighter. In winter also, a salwar is preferable because one can wear a woolen salwar and so keep the legs warm.

Even for cycling, playing games like tennis, hockey and any other sport, a salwar is very convenient. A girl wearing a white salwar, a white khameej and a white dupata looks just as smart as a girl in white shorts.

This Punjabi dress is not complete without a dupata. A dupata which is a sort of a long scarf thrown carelessly round the neck adds more charm to this dress.

These days as wearing of contrast colours is all the go, it is easy to keep in step with the fashion where salwar and khameej is concerned. A light coloured salwar, a contrast coloured khameej and then a dupatta to go with the salwar makes a perfect picture. Some ladies like to wear all the three pieces matching, the college girls usually wear a white cotton salwar, a printed khameej and a white dupatta. A number of girls use salwar and khameej as an evening dress because it is as comfortable as slack, as smart as skirts and as becoming as a saree.

So far as the welfare of Indian women is concerned, says Lakshmi Pandit, there is much that we can learn from Europe and America, but there is also a great deal that we can teach to the people of the West. But Russia has recently set new standards for the women of the world which we shall have to watch carefully. When Lakshmi formed contacts with Russian women in Europe she was much impressed by their heroism. I do not think it will be out of the picture to give the reader, while studying Indian women and Vijaya Lakshmi Pandit's views thereof, few significant facts concerning the Russian women, because the world has grown so short that in order to study things usefully, we must study them comparatively.

Names of many women famous for their high courage and indomitable spirits figure in Russian history; their characters have been immortalised in song and story. But even these great figures of the past pale before the heroism and self-sacrifice, the patriotism and courage displayed by Soviet women in the great Patriotic War.

The Soviet woman is a citizen with full rights in the Soviet State. She enjoys the same rights as men in all branches of the economic, state, cultural and social as well as political life of the country. In the USSR women have the same rights as men to guaranteed employment and payment for their work, to rest and leisure, to maintenance in old age or sickness, to education.

Over 1,700 women of various nationalities are Deputies to the Supreme Soviet of the USSR and Supreme Soviets of the Union and Autonomous Republics and 456,000 women are Deputies to the local Soviets of Workers' Deputies. Tens of thousands of Soviet women are managing plants, factories, institutions, collective farms; they are engaged in scientific, social and political activities. In 1940 there were 150,000 women engineers and technicians in the USSR. On the eve of the war half the students of the institutions of higher learning and special high schools were women. This complete equality with men in all spheres of life, which women enjoy in our country, has helped to develop their political activity and created initiatives.

Soviet women met the hard trials of war-time well prepared. Bred to uphold the high traditions of the Russian women of the past, inspired by selfless love of their Soviet homeland, they rose to the defence of their country with their fathers, husbands, brothers and sons. With arms in their hands, they fought side by side with men in the ranks of the glorious Red Army; they fought heroically, fearlessly, not sparing their lives and displaying equal courage and bravery as well as military skill. In the rear, women workers in factories and plants, in collective farm fields, worked untiringly, producing armaments, ammunitions, equipment and provisions for the Red Army.

The following figures may suffice to illustrate the heroism and valour of Soviet women. By February 1, of the current year over 72,000 awards had been conferred on women for gallantry in action. In the course of the war forty-four women won the high title of Hero of the Soviet Union and three that of Hero of Socialist Labour. Many thousands of women were with partisan detachments; about 8,000 have been decorated with the medal of Partisan of the Great Patriotic War.

INSTANCES OF VALOUR

It is worth while to cite a few instances of the valour displayed by women in battle. Evdoki Nosal, junior lieutenant in the air force, who had been a pedagogue before the war, went to the front as a volunteer. She has 354 combat flights to her credit and has dropped 50,000 kilograms of bombs on the enemy. She was the first woman flyer to receive the title of Hero of the Soviet Union during the war.

The nurse Valerie Gnarovskaye saved lives of 300 wounded men. During a certain battle, when German tanks were approaching the head-quarters of the regiment, she took a bundle of handgrenades and threw herself under the Tiger. The enemy machine was blown up and this helped to repel the attack.

Thousands of similar examples could be cited. Names of Soviet girl partisans Zoya Kosmodemyanskaya and Liza Chaikina have become legendary.

The war put on the defence industry demands for a ceaseless supply of tanks, shells, bombs, planes and other armaments, and for equipment and provisions. The brunt of this titanic task of keeping the Red Army supplied unfailingly fell on the shoulders of the Soviet working women. Millions of women took their places for the first time at lathes, open hearth furnaces, oil drillers, at tillers of airplanes, locomotives, tractors and combines. In extremely brief periods of time they mastered complicated trades and professions in factories and plants, in mines and on railways. They invariably displayed resourcefulness and initiative in their work and refused to be intimidated by difficulties.

There is no Russian ideal which conflicts with the ideals of Vijaya Lakshmi. She also wants the Indian women to be famous for high courage and indomitable strength. The character of Indian women in the past has been immortalised in story and song, for example there is Sita, Rani of Jhansi and many others, and Vijaya Lakshmi with her band is working for golden age of the future in India. And we have no doubt that the name of Lakhsmi will be immortalised in story and song. In fact she has already done enough in America to merit that unique honour. When India becomes free, we have no doubt that the women trained by leaders like Mrs. Pandit will display self-sacrifice and heroism in the pariotic war. In fact the Rani of Jhansi Regiment under Subhas Bose has already astonished the world.

Lakshmi also wants the Indian women to be a citizen with full rights enjoyed by men. She wants men and women to be equal in all branches of economic, political, social, and cultural life. Indian women if given such a status can certainly meet any danger from any frontiers of India. They can fight shoulder to shoulder with the male members of their family. That is what Lakshmi wants the Indian women to do. She wants them to be inspired by the high ideals. They should stand up to defend their homeland in peace and war. Indian women can fight, violently or non-violently, heroically and fearlessly. There is nothing which the Russian women have done and Indian women will fail to do in Free India.

NAWAB SALAR JUNG BAHADUR

The restle ideasss of Lakshmi are summed up in the following quotations. She wants the Indian women to rise up with a jump :—

(1) " The world has had enough of injustice, enough of hunger and misery, and all those things that

drag a man's soul to the very gates of despair and tragedy, and from every corner of the globe comes the cry to demolish a structure which allows such things to be, and to replace it by some thing new based on the principles of truth, fair-play and justice."

(2) " ......to each person comes a time when there is a conflict of duties and loyalties, and if the path I have chosen is not the right one, my children will forgive me because they love me and are my friends."

(3) " I am one of those fortunate individuals who have always been able to get a thrill out of life and I can honestly say, the occasions when I have been bored have been exceedingly rare."

(4) " The interest of our country demands our unity in face of a common growing danger. Let us not hold back, because remember—If India dies who lives? If India lives who dies ?"

(5) " We may still be behind other nations, but the dawn breaks and the first bright rays are stealing over the country giving hope to many weary hearts ...... India would live and her future would grow into a glorious thing."

VI

THE MODEL HOME

In order to have model women, we must have model homes. The chief advantage that Vijaya Lakshmi have had was the congenial home provided by her father for the family. The rise of the Nehrus can be directly traced to the Anand

Bhawan which made thinking possible in the right royal rational manner. The magnificent rooms, the spacious lawns, the cool consoling tank, and the sense of freedom from financial worries, coupled with vigorous education at home under trained governesses, was an ideal college for the Nehru children—and there it was that Jawaharlal, Vijaya Lakshmi, and Krishna were brought up by a father who himself was ahead of his times in India. When the girls went out on ponies, which no other parents would dare countenance, they were making experiments in the deserts of Indian orthodoxy. Having shaken off the leaden weight of social pebbles, they crossed the sea into the very den of the British lion and learnt to ride on his mane.

Anand Bhawan has given to Nehru sisters sweet memories like roses in December. Their memories of the past are all beautiful. They bring them the fragrance of happy flowers. The young Nehrus have memories of pleasant days, days of sunshine and laughter. But they also have memories of sad days when the sun seemed to be shadowed overhead by dark clouds and the life seemed barren. These are the memories of the days, when the family entered politics and sacrificed everything for the cause of the country.

" Memories," says Krishna, " that sadden the heart and tax to breaking point, for the old house is no longer what it was..................".

Sufferings of the Nehru family are well known. With a sudden turn of circumstances a house brimming with giggling laughters, was turned into a lonely one. It was constantly subjected to police raids. Most atrocious offences were committed by the government. The inmates suffered imprisonments. Pangs of separation was their lot. But disease and death didn't budge them from the path which they had confidently chosen. But for an exceptionally stronger will to work and win, the Nehrus would have probably been prostrated before the furious forces of the bullish bureaucracy.

Mrs. Vijaya Lakshmi Pandit has richly inherited her characteristic will to win from her father whose courage and determination none could excel. Constant endeavour to overcome difficulties and dangers provided her with opportunities of getting thrill from life. In an autobiographical study she writes :

" Difficulties, opposition, criticism, these things are meant to be overcome and there is a special joy in facing them and coming out on top. It is only when there is nothing but praise that life loses its charm and I begin to wonder, 'what I should do about it'! "

Lakshmi doesn't very much appreciate the soft life and easy-going principles. These fortunately have not constituted a trait in Nehru politics ever since the political movement possessed them.

In moments of calm reflection she is disappointed to find that our officials are tainted by a morbid desire for self-enjoyment for its own sake, irrespective of its national results. Self-abnregation with our nationalists has become due to prolonged practice a second nature. We have largely to blame the terroristic Government which has constantly been suppressing all political aspirations and persecuting the patriots. We have to thank our own philosophy of life, so deep-rooted in the soul, as a perfect weapon of national honour. Mrs. Vijaya Laxmi Pandit has suffered for the cause of India's freedom as much as any other leader of her rank. She has always avoided pleasure when there were means for that, but refused to make a willing martyr of herself. In April 1943 while she was in jail she loved to sleep inside the barracks in sympathy with other prisoners, who were not allowed to sleep out side, but she did not, as her delicate health would not permit her. In her diary she writes :

"First class prisoners are now permitted to sleep out but Indu and Purnima are remaining inside the barrack on account of Vimla who is a second-class prisoner. I thought it foolish to make a martyr of myself when my health is so poor, and have been sleeping outside." So she refused to be a martyr on purely sentimental grounds. An intimate observation of her mode of living makes it clear that she not only lives but makes every moment of her life alive. In battling against obstacles lies for members of the Nehru family, the golden path and the principle of politics.

In addition to the rigour of personality and vigour of philosophy her personal charm has been a great asset to her in contributing to her success in the public career. She thrilled the American people with her speeches. The Yanks, the Negroes and foreigners in U. S. A. listened to her with rapt attention. What blazed their interest was no doubt the humaneness of India's cause. Her impressive personality and beautiful oratory fascinated her cultured audience.

Her personal charm attracted them no less. Under the heading 'her charm delights her listeners' an English Daily of India, dated April 1945, reported :

"American interest in the problems of India has been lightened by the visit of Mrs. Vijaya Lakshmi Pandit, whose personal charm has delighted her listeners at a large number of public and private meetings."

Mrs. Krishna Hutheesing, her younger sister pays a remarkable tribute to Mrs. Vijaya Lakshmi Pandit :—

"From her childhood Swarup (family name of Mrs. Vijaya Lakshmi Pandit) had been a very tactful person and was eminently suited to become a minister. She seldom if ever gets agitated over anything and deals with all kinds of situations in a calm unruffled manner. Charming, self possessed and beautiful, she has little difficulty in winning people over. As a minister she was a great success. It was difficult task she undertook to perform never having been trained for any work of that type, but she excelled herself at it and was very popular. When Swarup started taking an active part in politics her ability as speaker surprised us all. She seemed to have been born to it and seldom showed any signs of nervousness no matter how large the gathering, which she had to address. She speakes with fluency and ease both in Hindustani and English.

" When she was still quite young, her hair had started to become grey—this is a hereditary trait running in the family. All too rapidly her hair became white and yet more white. Now she has silvery white hair but this factor doesn't in any way take away her physical charm, on the contrary it adds to her loveliness.

" She is a capable mother and an efficient house-wife. In spite of the fact that politics take up a great deal of her time, she still finds time to look after her home and children."

As the Nehrus have been impoverished in gold, they have enriched themselves with the affection of their countrymen. But their house has still maintained dignity of a bygone age.

" I sat in the old familiar garden," says Krishna, " the only unchanged place in a world that is always changing. Before me stood the stately house that was my home, and I gazed at it with unseeing eyes, with my thoughts far away...... At my feet and round about, lovely butterflies flitted. The fresh smell of the grass was good and the scent of roses was wafted along the breeze towards me. I lay back with a sigh......"

So this is the house where Lakshmi was born and brought up. It is a large rambling building which was once full of people. It had every luxury that taste and money could provide. Its master, Pandit Motilal, was a fine-looking gentleman with a tremendous personality. He seemed to fill the whole house with his presence. His laughter echoed in the house. His love surrounded the family. He was a tower of strength to his children. The lady of the house flitted about looking after family.

" Everywhere there was life and activity—happiness and contentment," says Krishna, " and in such an atmosphere three children grew up."

Jawaharlal, Vijaya Lakshmi and Krishna grew up together in this happy atmosphere. While the father was yet alive, the family bade goodbye to pomp and splendour and lavish grandeur. They adopted simplicity as the creed of their life. But they were not downcast. The hearty laughter of Motilal still rang in the house and lit up every heart with cheerfulness. And when the Great Man died in the thick of the battle for India's freedom, Jawaharlal had already filled the gap in the front line. Lakshmi Pandit and Krishna looked up to him to light their way in the night of domestic and national difficulties.

Jawaharlal's personal guidance has influenced the activity of his sisters. Besides the natural ties of a brother, he has also been a philosopher, and friend to his sisters. 'Bhai' has played an important part in Vijaya Lakshmi's life. It is manifest in her book " Prison Days " which is a diary of her recent imprisonment.

" 10th November 1942. Bhaiya Duj day to-day. How many anniversaries of this day I have spent apart from Bhai......the last day or two I have been very vividly reminded of my childhood days and all the later period from adolescence onwards. Bhai has played such an important part in my life. Out of the many good things fate gave me at my birth, one of the best was surely my brother, to have known and loved him and been so near to him would have been ample justification for having been born".

Thus she expresses the depth of her love for her brother in beautiful words and feelings more profound than a hectic praise.

Jawahar Lal's younger sister Mrs. Krishna Hutheesingh in her book *With No Regret* pines for a reversal of the time span so that she could once again live the moments spent by her in company of her brother and father.

Fascinatingly she describes her tour in Europe with Jawahar Lal in the year 1925. In the course of the tour they visited England, France, Switzerland, Belgium, Germany and Russia. Jawahar took his little sister round visiting museums, art galleries, and other places of historical interest. They avoided theatres. He introduced her to the eminent personalities of the age, including Romain Rolland, Ernst Toller, Chicherin, the then Russian Foreign minister, and Einstein the great scientist. Amongst the meetings attended were the meetings of the League Against Imperialism held in Brussels, the 10th anniversary celebrations of the Russian Revolution, and a huge state of banquet at Moscow, where Krishna had her taste of Vodka.

Vijaya Lakshmi Pandit too has been to Europe. She has gathered in her person considerable experience of the international social and political movements.

This is the background of the intellectual development of Nehru sisters. There are extracts in Jawahar Lal's letters to his sisters, which give us an insight of the broad vision of this great man of the age. They also speak of the affection and care he has for his sisters.

Once perchance he was arrested on a date which was his sister's birthday when he contemplated sending a present to her. He was very sorry when he could not do that.

VII

THE NEHRU SISTERS

Krishna Hatheesing cherishes sweet memories of her sister, Mrs. Vijaya Lakshmi Pandit. The former describes the feelings of the sisters when Jawaharlal was arrested for the first time as follows :—

" In one corner of the room sat the elder daughter of the house (Vijaya Lakshmi). She was married and had children and realized fully how much anguish her parents must be feeling. Her eyes were glued to their faces anxiously and her heart was torn with pain to watch their silent suffering and to be able to help. In another part of the room, leaning up against the wall with her head turned away from others, stood the younger daughter. In her heart there was an ache also, in her eyes were unshed tears, and her mind was seething with rebellious thoughts."

Mrs. Krishna Hatheesing touchingly describes the arrest of Mrs. Vijaya Lakshmi Pandit and that of her own. It is the story of the sisters' first visit to the British prison :—

"Time marched on. The old house had seen many changes and it had still to see many more. Cars stood along the drive and policemen were dotted all over the compound. All these preparations were for the arrest of two daughters. They had not sat idle all these years but had worked and followed in their father's footsteps, and upheld the tradition of their family. And for this they too had to go to prison as their father and brother before. Courteously the officers produced the warrant, smiling the girls received it and turned to go inside to collect a few belongings Just then the little mother came, as fast as her weak limbs could carry her.

'What is all this about? She asked, 'why so many cars and people?'

"Gently the elder daughter (Lakshmi Pandit) put her arm round the mother and told her. For a moment she weakened and tears filled her eyes as she clasped her daughters and whispered.

'I shall be so lonely without you.'

But it was only for a moment. She straightened her tiny figure and faced this new ordeal with all the courage of a baffled lioness.

'I am proud of you,' she said, 'very proud.'

'And I am not too old to follow suit,' she added with a twinkle in her eyes.

"She clasped her daughters once again and put out her hands to give them her blessings. But that delicate wisp of a body had undergone too much suffering and anguish, and could bear no more. The girls were driven away in a car to their destination......And life went on as usual.

"A prison cell with dark grim walls, within which sat two sisters—drawn closer together now than ever before, with a common bond. They sat leaning against each other, looking through the iron bars at a beautiful red sky which meant a glorious sunset somewhere, beyond those prison walls. Wrapped up in thoughts they sat, one (Vijaya Lakshmi) longing for her own home, her husband and the little children she had left behind! the other longing to hear the infectious laughter of her father's that never failed to give courage and hope, and to feel the beloved mother's arms round her—the mother who was left alone in a big dreary house.

"There was a rattling of chains and clanging of doors. What was it all about, prisoners wondered. A wardress came towards the sisters—a telegram in her hands. Fearfully they took it, then after a second they smiled at each other. So she had kept her word, their brave little mother, and she too was behind prison bars in some distant prison. How very courageous of her, and how ruthless of them that took her—an old woman of sixty-five!"

VIII

MENACE OF EMPIRE

No wondor, the well-knit and well-bred Nehru family has grown to be a menace to the British Empire. Every Nehru is reponsible for this menace, but the major part has been played by Motilal, Jawaharlal, and Vijaya Lakshmi. How Vijaya Lakshmi has been a menace to the Empire in U. S. A. has already been detailed out in the previous chapter. A beautiful essay on the subject by K. Rama Rao is reproduced below from the *Tribune* dated April 8, 1945 :—

'A domestic event, however, just then absorbed my attention. This was the birth of a little sister. I had long nourished a secret grievance at not having any brothers or sisters when everybody else seemed to have them, and the prospect of having at last a baby brother or sister all to myself was exhilarating. Father was then in Europe. I remember waiting anxiously in the verandah for the event. One of the doctors came and told me of it and added, presumably as a joke, that I must be glad that it was not a boy who would have taken a share in my patrimony. I felt bitter and angry at the thought that any one should imagine that I could harbour such a vile notion.'

* * * *

"Mrs. Vijaya Lakshmi Pandit was born in the middle of the Boer War when the British were having the worst of it. I do not mean to say that Baby Vijaya Lakshmi caused all that trouble, but if they had known that one day she was going to develop into a menace to the British Empire, a Herod-like Lieutenant-Governor might have been awake and alert about an obvious portent of disaster. Pandit Jawaharlal Nehru, who describes the happy event in his life-story is the least envious of men and the most loving of brothers. In jail to-day he must be feeling very proud of his sister's work in the United States. The common patrimony they have is national service and national reputation.

"Don Iddon, the New York correspondent of the London 'Daily Mail' who has described Mrs. Pandit as a menace to the empire in a message to his paper, has used language which he must have conceived to be the most appropriate for the occasion, but which comes aptly from the lips of Englishmen dead drunk or thoroughly enraged. He does not like 'the spectacle of this woman going from town to town addressing huge audiences and stirring up anti-British feeling, a spectacle not calculated to improve Anglo-American team work.' That patriarch of Toryism, Sir Alfred Knox, wanted to know from Mr. Amery what the British Information Services were doing about it. But Mr. Amery contented himself with the mock-righteous reflection that the American public must have already assessed 'her obviously fantastic assertions at their true value,' these assertions being that India was a vast concentration camp, and was indeed without the religious differences on which the British have been banking for maintaining their tottering Empire. According to a Free Press cable, British officials in the U.S.A., adopted some counter tactics, which, however, failed to produce the desired effect.

The India Office approached Sir B.P. Singh Roy to undertake a lecture tour of America, but he has declined the offer on the ground of ill-health—that diplomatic cloak for basic unwillingness to do unpleasant work for English imperialists abroad. Mr. Amery should have gone on with Sir Girja Shankar Pajpai and T.A. Raman.

WAR IS ENDING, BUT WHAT ABOUT PEACE ?

"True to her name, Mrs. Pandit has always enjoyed abundant good luck in her political career, which unlike several others, though similarly fortunate, she has sustained by brilliant ability and character. It strikes, me that, when she went to the United States, she did not mean to undertake serious political work. When I met her in Sevagram in September last, she appeared to be still worried about her passport. I did not get from her the idea that she had been charged with any mission. I pressed on her one or two questions and almost took a bet with her that she would not be able to resist the temptation of plunging into a political campaign almost without knowing it. I was acting on a journalist's instinct for big game. At any rate, both the United Provinces Government and the Central Government seem to have satisfied themselves that she was not the person to set the prairies of the United States on fire, otherwise they would not have given her the passport. She went there as a mother to see her children, but the mother has been submerged by the politician and the patriot in her. She got going famously almost the next moment she landed. And it was a psychological moment, too. The war was approaching its end, but what about the peace that endureth ? Bretton Woods and Dumbarton Oaks were bad enough, but the Pacific Relations Conference did not prove materially better, though it provided the Indian delegation with a platform from which to thunder against colonialism. Anglo-American differences had been widening with the near termination of hostilities. The monstrous lie of Congress being Fascist and Totalitarian, which gullible Americans swallowed in August and September, 1942, has died under the weight of its own iniquity. The Trade Delegation from India did some spade work for the next campaign, and so have the gallant band of patriotic Indians led by Sridhant and J. J. Singh. Mrs. Pandit thus caught the tide at its high flood.

SHE HAS PLEADED FOR UNIVERSALISATION OF FREEDOM

"If the British propagandist chiefs wish to put an end to the menace to their empire, they will do well to bottle up other outlets of expression as well. It is not only on the platform that Mrs. Pandit has been victorious. She has been lunching with the high and dining with the mighty. She is a much-interviewed person. Leader-writers have found their task made easy by her stimulating talk. Anyway, newspapers find her a good front-page feature. It is perhaps by her radio talks that she has captured the American audiences, and I have no doubt in my mind that, with her charming voice and her lucid expression, she bids fair to rival Franklin Dala Roosevelt himself, the best radio-speaker in America. Mrs. Pandit is by no means an orator like Mrs. Naidu. She cannot have the patience either to sit down to 'argue' a case and 'make out points.' In this respect she is exactly like her brother. She has, however, a certain authentic capacity for clearly approaching a problem and putting it impressively before her audience. In the present campaign she has lifted political issues to Sinaitic heights, reminding us of the oratory that lives because it is touched up to moral issues. She has pleaded for the universalisation of freedom; she has pleaded for an atmosphere of faith in Indo-British relations. Is Britain sincere? If so, why is Jawaharlal Nehru in jail? Why then does the constitutional deadlock continue? Does Britain mean business? How will you fight Japan effectively with an unreconciled India as a base? In the land of Abraham Lincon, India's missionary did not find it necessary to preach against Pakistan, to ridicule threats of civil war, to ridicule an empire quarter free and three-fourths slave, to ridicule a colonialism that has been outmoded, that has led to wars in the past which the Americans condemn, but the British would cherish and keep. The greatest service that Mrs. Pandit has done by her campaign is to have fixed up India in the focus of the world at a critical time when great decisions are being forged. India is no longer Britain's domestic concern but an international issue, one of those issues which must be answered, answered at once and answered aright. San Francisco is in sight. The Mudaliars and the Noons may be depended upon to deliver to the conference a packet of lies. Mrs. Pandit is there to watch them and to expose them."

IX

THE STRUGGLE GOES ON

Returning home from America, Mrs. Vijaya Lakshmi Pandit has picked up the threads of the struggle for India's freedom. Having won battles abroad, she came to India like a seasoned commander-in-chief. Directly she stood for elections and was returned unopposed to the United Provinces Legislative Assembly. Again she has been elevated to a position in the cabinet, and has been appointed a minister. Perhaps, she will take up the same old portfolio of Health and Hygiene, and take up the schemes which she could not materialize due to political atmosphere. Again we will find her in her chair in the Secretariat. The history will repeat itself, but it will not be the same history.

Not only is India nearer to the goal of freedom, but also Vijaya Lakshmi has her views considerably galvanized in

America. Her address at Allahabad on February 3, 1946 was an illuminating one.

Mrs. Vijayalaxmi Pandit addressing a public meeting stressed the need of organisations built all over the world to tell the real conditions of India and its political life to the world. We do not want any propaganda to be done through these organisations.

India's conditions do not need any propaganda, they only need telling of true facts, asserted Mrs. Pandit. She criticised the vile propaganda done by the British in America against India and said that this was keeping the world dark about India and necessitated our telling the world true facts. Mrs. Pandit had no doubt that when the people of the world were told true facts. they reacted favourably to that, and understood the falsity of wrong impressions created in them at the cost of thousands of dollars.

Mrs. Pandit also told the gathering of her meeting with President Truman to find out his views on the Indian questions, but was sorry to say that no clear answer was given by him on this question.

Mrs. Pandit narrated at length the San Francisco Conference and the setting in which it was held. She said that though the representatives of India were included in the conference they were men whom the British Government had chosen for their own selfish ends. The British Government wanted to increase one more vote in the conference in their favour and interest. As such, said Mrs. Pandit, when she sent a memorandum to the conference detailing the real situation of the country since 1942 and making it clear that the representatives sent to the conference were not the representatives of the people of India, it created a stir. This stir was caused in the conference, added Mrs. Pandit, because she had told the truth and that too with the voice of millions of people of India behind her.

Referring to the work done at the conference, Mrs. Pandit compared it with the puppet's dance and said every nation that had assembled viewed each other with suspicion. The real issues were never touched upon. Only superficial things were considered at the conference and as such the structure for bringing peace to the world was never built. Even the foundation for it was not laid.

Mrs. Pandit asserted that as long as half the world was dominated by imperialism, there could be no peace and prosperity in the world. There could be no security in the world as long as only things concerning the unity of Big Four were considered, for world security and peace it was necessary that solid foundation for every nation's freedom must be laid, she said.

Mrs. Vijayalaxmi Pandit referred to the word inter-dependence used at the San Francisco Conference and ridiculed the Indian representatives to the conference also singing the same note of inter-dependence. How could any country be inter-dependent with another unless it was independent itself, asked Mrs. Pandit. The dependence of two countries on each other can only bear results when they are independent in themselves. It was, therefore, necessary that all countries in the world should be independent if inter-dependence had to play any important role in bringing peace and security to the world.

Mrs. Pandit emphasised that unless a conference such as called at San Fransisco had the character of equality of its members, it was a farce to call such conference and waste of money and energy. A conference devoid of these two essential things could not bring peace and prosperity to the world. •

Mrs. Pandit also felt that the new world which was being evolved after the war, was one of jealousy and strife and not of peace and prosperity.

X

WINNING THE PEACE

We have won the war, says Vijaya Lakshmi, but we have miserably failed to win peace. And it is towards that end that the energies of sincere statesmen must be directed. In that picture India and her leaders will fill the central pivot. It is there that Vijaya Lakshmi will earn another bunch of laurels at the hands of her countrymen.

But in order to win peace for the world, says Mrs. Pandit, India must first win freedom for herself. We must have independence before we can think of inter-dependence. India has now a threefold mission in the world: first, to free herself; secondly, to free other countries; and thirdly, to bind all the countries in an unbreakable brotherhood.

That is the mission of Vijaya Lakshmi, because it is the mission of Mahatma Gandhi, and the mission of Mahatma Gandhi is of course the mission of India.

REVIEWS AND OPINIONS

TEACHINGS OF MAHATMA GANDHI

The essence of wisdom for all those who seek inspiration from the teachings of Mahatma Gandhi will be found in this book. —*The Hindustan Review.*

It is at times difficult to acquaint himself with Mr. Gandhi's views on a particular subject. This is exactly where the book under review comes in handy.

—*The Illustrated Weekly.*

This book will enable the reader to follow the evolution of Gandhiji's thought on the subjects dealt with.

—*The Pioneer.*

Mr. Jag Parvesh is well-known as a painstaking and conscientious literary editor and author. The author's devoted study of Gandhiji's writings has enabled him to accomplish his work with discrimination.

— N. JOG—*The Bombay Chronicle.*

The book well merits being called a Dictionary of Gandhism. —*The Indian Express.*

Mr. Jag Parvesh has handled the great mass of material with rare skill, and makes of it a book which is not only authoritative, but also eminently readable. —*The Tribune.*

To students of Gandhian literature the book is bound to be a serviceable publication. —*The Hindu.*

For a reference book on Gandhiji's teachings the book is hard to beat. NAWAB SALAR JUNG BAHADUR —*Sunday Times.*

THE UNSEEN POWER

Every word of it deserves to be read, re-read and pondered over, for they show us the way to Truth, and to freedom from worries and troubles. —*The Searchlight.*

Contemporary thought is the richer and fuller for this little booklet. —*Young Ceylon.*

Mr. Jag Parvesh Chander's labour has conduced to the production of a work of great value to all seekers after higher thought and spiritual knowledge. —*Hindustan Review.*

It should adorn every library in India for it is the *Bible* of present day Indian thought which will influence the world after the horrors of the present war. —*Sind Observer.*

The book provides an inspiring message to those who are worried upon the troubled scene of the modern world. —*Hindustan Standard.*

The perusal of this book should bring about a great change in our religious and moral attitude. —*Calcutta Review.*

The entire work is characterised by moral and spiritual elevation that it is bound to offer solace to the most cynical in their tribulations. —*Indian Express.*